# MARTIAL ARTS
# FOR
# KIDS

Dear Dave & Ellen,

I'ts amazing after all the years we've talked about doing this book that it has become a reality. Thanks to the both of you for all your support you've given to me. Let our relationship continue to grow and our families remain close so we can enjoy our lives together.

Norman &
JESSICA

# MARTIAL ARTS
# FOR
# KIDS

The Road to Inner Strength,
Self-Awareness,
and a Peaceful World

## RICHARD DEVENS &
## NORMAN SANDLER

**WEATHERHILL**
NEW YORK • TOKYO

To all those embarked upon the special journey into the world of martial arts. If you strive for a synthesis of the mental, physical, and spiritual components of your being, with an attitude of respect, understanding, and love, then you will have captured the essence of the martial arts, and the world will be a better place.

First edition, 1997
Published by Weatherhill, Inc., of New York and Tokyo, with editorial offices at 568 Broadway, Suite 705, New York, N.Y. 10012. Protected by copyright under the terms of the International Copyright Union; all rights reserved. Except for fair use in book reviews, no part of this book may be reproduced for any reason by any means, including any method of photographic reproduction, without permission of Weatherhill, Inc.

Cover photographs by Stephanie Talmadge and Felicia Lebow, Hi-Tech Photography, Plainview and Great Neck, N.Y.

Library of Congress Cataloging-in-Publication Data
Devens, Richard.
    Martial arts for kids / by Richard Devens and Norman Sandler —1st ed.
            p.          cm.
    Includes bibliographical references.
    ISBN 0-8340-0401-8 (softcover)
    1. Martial arts. 2. Martial arts for children. I. Sandler, Norman (Norman Lee)
GV 1101.D48    1997
613.7' 148—dc21                              97-28591
                                                  CIP

# CONTENTS

*While parents might choose ballet or gymnastics or an organized sport to help their child develop correct posture, attitude, and discipline, those activities might not help the child with life outside the ballet studio, gym, or playing field . . . Martial arts not only support physical and mental development but supply a base of knowledge that can be brought by children to all their activities, throughout the day and night; it is knowledge that applies to all aspects of their lives.*

—**Ernie George**
seventh-degree black belt, kenpo

# ACKNOWLEDGMENTS

The authors wish to thank all those who so generously shared their special knowledge with us. Dr. Marc Abrams was introduced to us by Dr. Amy Cohen Anneling, a psychologist and a cousin of one of the authors. Knowing we were working on this book, she thought he might be helpful, and he certainly was. Dr. Abrams is a psychologist and a martial artist, and the treatment of children comprises over half his practice.

Thanks also to Howard Frydman, a third-degree black belt in shotokan karate, former captain of the U.S.A. Maccabiah Team, and a member of the U.S.A. International A.A.U. Karate Fighting Team from 1977 through 1982. Now owner of a school in Port Washington, New York, he has extensive teaching experience, especially with children. Ernie George, a seventh-degree black belt in kenpo known for his extraordinary stances, provided the epigraph at the front of this book. His fitting statement clearly explains why the study of a martial art can be so beneficial to children.

Dr. Steven Handwerker, a psychologist and martial artist, made important contributions to the "Self-Discipline" chapter, as did Kathy Owen, who holds a fifth-degree black belt in kenpo and owns a school in Newark, Delaware, where a large number of her students are children. Her advice on choosing a school and instructor, as well as her thoughts on the subject of what particular systems are better for particular body types, were both very illuminating.

Dr. Stanley Katz, chief of the Division of Cardiology and director of the Cardiac Catherization Laboratory at North Shore University Hospital, Manhasset, New York, took time from his busy schedule to offer his insights on fitness, and to clear up some misconceptions regarding the heart. When the recording of our interview was lost due to a malfunctioning tape, he graciously granted us another one. He also proofread the transcript of the interview to ensure that no mistakes crept in.

Dr. Robert E. Schwartz, an orthopedic surgeon and section chief of the Research Division of Orthopedic Surgery, North Shore University Hospital, Manhasset, New York, provided us with information which we utilized in "The Doctors Speak." Other important contributors to this chapter were: Dr. Daniel L. Kraus, a chiropractor with a black belt in judo and extensive wrestling experience; Dr. Roger Russell, a chiropractic orthopedist and kenpo instructor with a fifth-degree black belt; Dr. Stanley Weindorf, a pediatrician; and Dr. Ellen Sandler, a chiropractor with a background in martial arts and dance. Her comments regarding posture, as well as her comparison of dance, gymnastics, and martial arts, were quite useful.

Thanks to Thomas Festa, a fifth-degree black belt in tae kwon do, a teacher since 1975, and owner of a martial arts school in Franklin Square, New York. A competitor on the local and national circuit for nearly two decades, his insights greatly enhanced the chapter "Choosing an Instructor and School," as did those of Robert E. Walzer, a practitioner of aikido and owner of the only full-time aikido academy in Queens, New York, whose students he graciously allowed us to interview.

Much information for this key chapter was also provided by Jack Krystek, owner of a judo, jujutsu, and boxing school in Ozone Park, New York. Jack also holds a Ph.D. in Holistic Health Sciences and has been working with kids for more than thirty years.

Thanks also to Christina Muccini, a three-time junior national karate champion, a four-time adult national karate champion, and a bronze medalist in the Pan American Games, for her contribution to "Martial Arts and Competition." This chapter also benefited from the insights of Tokey Hill, the 1980 World Union Karate-do Organization (W.U.K.O.) champion and current U.S. National Team coach, whose accomplishments have been duly noted in the *Guinness Book of World Records.*

We also wish to thank Robin Rielly, a sixth-degree black belt in shotokan, and the most senior student of Teruyuki Okazaki Sensei, eighth-degree black belt, head of the I.S.K.F. (International Shotokan Karate Federation), and vice-chairman of the J.K.A. (Japan Karate Association). Thanks also to Gilbert Velez, who was for sixteen years the private student of the late kenpo senior grandmaster, Ed Parker. Mr. Velez holds an eighth-degree black belt and owns a school in Tucson, Arizona. Of all kenpo practitioners, his movements, punctuated with incredible kenpo "explosions," most closely resemble those of his illustrious teacher.

A special thanks also to all the parents we interviewed. They all have recognized the value of martial arts training, and because of this, their children are very fortunate. And last, but certainly not least, we want to thank the children, who really provided the inspiration for this book.

# PREFACE

When this book was conceived, it was our intention to write about a topic that to our knowledge had never been addressed in book form. There have been articles about martial arts for children, and books for children dealing with specific systems. However, we wanted to provide a broad overview of the benefits that children can derive from the study of any martial art. The fact that specific styles or systems are occasionally given as examples in no way implies that they are more beneficial than any other.

A few words concerning the title are in order: In a discussion with a third party, we were told that what we were writing was not about martial arts for kids; for our title to be accurate, the children themselves would have to be able to read it. In a manner of speaking, our critic is correct, but to write such a book was never our intention. The fact that a parent might be inspired by the book to take a four-year-old to karate class, to our minds shows that our work is intended *for* kids. At the same time, however, we tried to present the material in a simple, straightforward style so that many children will be able to read it. This, we hope, will encourage discussions between them and their parents about the issues raised. On the other hand, the title was not meant to imply that the information discussed is applicable only to children. All the benefits discussed can be reaped by people of all ages.

We chose to focus on kids because kids grow into adults, and it is our belief that through martial arts, they can be better adults. Other factors being equal, the earlier one begins to study a particular discipline (when the muscles and reflexes are still developing), the better. The martial arts provide a cornucopia of benefits, including better coordination, flexibility, strength, self-discipline, confidence, and heightened powers of concentration. It may be argued that ballet, gymnastics, piano lessons, or ice skating will also provide such benefits, but we feel that none of these is capable of providing the "total package" of physical, mental, and spiritual benefits that the martial arts offer. And while we would never insist that studying a martial art is better for a child than another activity, we will argue that the benefits to be derived are indisputable, and can enhance a child's performance in other pursuits.

On the other hand, we do not believe that children should be forced to participate in martial arts study, or in any of the activities mentioned. With so many to choose from, there is no reason why children should not be allowed to participate in activities they like. Discovering and engaging in such pursuits can be a source of endless satisfaction, and it is certainly better to have a happy young gymnast or violinist in the family than a miserable and resentful karate student.

A note regarding editorial style: Some martial arts have become so familiar—judo, for example—that their names are considered English words, while others are considered foreign terms, and thus italicized. To avoid confusion, the principle martial arts discussed in this book—kenpo, karate, shotokan, jujutsu, aikido, kung fu, jeet kune do, and t'ai chi ch'uan—will appear in Roman type, as will the proper names of schools and two key terms used throughout (except on first mention): dojo and kata. Other foreign terms appear in italics. Also, although we sometimes refer to a child as "he" or "she," all the advice and information provided here, unless specifically stated otherwise, applies to girls as well as boys. Although we have conformed to the editorial custom of using the masculine pronoun "he" to refer to children or students, the techniques and skills of the martial arts do not depend upon great size and strength, and progress can be made, and benefits realized, by anyone, regardless of age, sex, or physique. We heartily recommend martial arts practice to all.

# INTRODUCTION

*Karate-do is a noble martial art, and the reader can rest assured that those who take pride in breaking boards or smashing tiles, or who boast of being able to perform outlandish feats like stripping flesh or plucking out ribs, really know nothing about karate. They are playing around in the leaves and branches of a great tree, without the slightest concept of the trunk.*

—Gichin Funakoshi
founder of shotokan karate

Although the Asian martial arts have been around for centuries, their penetration into the popular consciousness is a relatively recent phenomenon. Forty years ago, many people thought of them as mystical arts of the exotic East. Their practitioners were thought of as strange creatures who could break boards with their bare hands and apply secret holds that would paralyze opponents. However, through increasing East-West contact, more Westerners became involved in the practice of these arts and their names and styles became more familiar on this side of the Pacific. Their popularity grew, until schools and instructors of judo, karate, aikido, and tae kwon do are now everywhere. The Martial Arts Business Association estimates that today over three million boys and girls under the age of eighteen practice a martial art regularly, and the number is growing rapidly.

## Martial Arts and the Media

The media, TV and the movies in particular, have been instrumental in popularizing the martial arts. Although the first movie we remember seeing specifically featuring martial arts was *The Five Fingers of Death* (1973), by that time martial arts had been shown on TV for at least a decade. Two very popular television series from the 1960s were *The Avengers,* in which Emma Peel (Diana Rigg) displayed her karate skills, and *The Green Hornet,* in which the Hornet's loyal sidekick Kato (Bruce Lee) regularly chopped down evil-doers. The charismatic Bruce Lee probably did more than anyone to bring the martial arts to the attention of the general public, both through his role as Kato and in his movies of the early 1970s, especially The *Chinese Connection* (aka *The Big Boss,* now a cult classic), and *Enter the Dragon.* Lee paved the way for the martial arts film superstars of today: Jackie Chan, Chuck Norris, Steven Seagal, Jean-Claude Van Damme, and Jeff Speakman.

Taking their cue from the popularity of these martial artists who became actors, famous actors and actresses have also incorporated martial arts in their movie roles. As British secret agent 007, Sean Connery displayed martial arts in the James Bond movies: in *Goldfinger* (1964), he traded judo throws with Honor Blackman, and in *You Only Live Twice* (1967) he trained as a *ninja,* the black-clad Japanese assassins of legend. Even after relinquishing his role as Bond, Connery continued to use martial arts in such films as *Rising Sun* (1993), a thriller that drew heavily on Eastern philosophy and culture. In one movie or another, many Hollywood stars have used martial arts to heighten the level of excitement, including Renee Russo, Sharon Stone, Sylvester Stallone, Michelle Pfeiffer, Wesley Snipes, Arnold Schwarzenegger, and Mel Gibson. Even famous people who are not actors have performed martial arts on the screen: Kareem Abdul-Jabbar clashed with Bruce Lee in *Game of Death* (1978), and kenpo senior grandmaster Ed Parker used martial arts as a hired assassin out to kill Peter Sellers in the comedy *Revenge of the Pink Panther* (1972).

Besides the popular Hollywood productions that appear in theaters, the martial arts films have a substantial "direct-to-video" market, in which Don "The Dragon" Wilson and Cynthia Rothrock have huge followings. As two out of the four top sales performers in the videocassette market, they were the recipients of *Time* magazine's first "direct-to-video" Oscars in the August 1996 issue.

However, the entertainment industry has also done the martial arts a disservice. Aside from being action-packed and displaying amazing feats of physical prowess, most films have offered little in the way of good acting, and the plots usually focus on the same old theme—getting revenge, usually in the most violent way possible. While it is true that action heroes such as Sylvester Stallone and Arnold Schwarzenegger must always be grievously wronged before they decide to take action, the number of people they wind up killing can only be described as excessive. In addition, much of the choreographed fighting techniques, such as very high kicks, would not be practical in real-life combat.

One notable exception in films is *The Karate Kid,* in which the character of Mr. Miyagi (Noriyuki "Pat" Morita) was based on that of a real-life Okinawan karate master. The kindly Miyagi teaches martial arts skills, but mostly self-confidence, to a troubled teenager (Ralph Macchio). The movie focuses on moral behavior, nonviolence, humility, and dedication to an ideal as a way of life. It is also very informative, showing how the movements employed in everyday activities, such as waxing a car, can be utilized in actual self-defense techniques. Many of the children we spoke to singled out this movie as the one that inspired them to study martial arts.

On television, the series *Kung Fu* features a wandering Shaolin monk (David Carradine) for whom kung fu is not just a fighting art; following its precepts is a way of life. This series was so popular it has been followed up with a sequel series entitled *Kung Fu: The Legend Continues.* Similarly, in *Walker: Texas Ranger,* the lead character (Chuck Norris) stresses "doing the right thing" over simply paying back bad with bad. This popular series recently hit the top ten for all network shows three different times in a single year, and is currently the number one show in its time slot.

Finally, for the younger kids, there are animated martial arts. The ninja craze of the late 1980s and early 1990s brought the *Teenage Mutant Ninja Turtles* to both TV and the big screen. The *Power Rangers* were the next wave in television; they were a little silly for the older kids, but like the Ninja Turtles, their programs portrayed positive values. Now on television are the *W.M.A.C. Masters,* featuring choreographed tournament matches, in which contestants abide by the rules and display true sportsmanship. During its first season, it was rated the number one new syndicated television program for kids between the ages of six and seventeen, and is now broadcast in over one hundred markets throughout the United States.

What role does the media play in influencing a child's perception of the martial arts? Should parents worry about their children being exposed to "good" or "bad" or "real" or "fake" portrayals of martial arts? "I think the media is giving kids less credit than they're due," says world champion martial arts master and actor Chuck Norris. "Kids today are smart," he continues. "They know what is right and wrong. I've been teaching martial arts for many years, and have worked with kids as young as five. These kids know what is real and what is not real on the screen."

Still, as with all entertainment presented to children, parental supervision is strongly advised. For example, the pay-per-view "no holds barred" fighting shows like *The Ultimate Challenge* are not the way we would want to introduce children to the martial arts. Although perhaps no more violent than some other professional sports, these are primarily moneymaking ventures, in which the moral and spiritual aspects of the martial arts are not shown. Any of the better programs mentioned above would be more suitable for children.

In any case, children should be made aware that the purpose of martial arts study is not to beat other people up but to make the martial artist a better person. The values of the martial artist are dedication, harmony, humility, and compassion, and any program in which these values are not apparent is not an accurate portrayal of the martial arts.

## What is a Martial Artist?

The ultimate goal of all true martial artists is a synthesis of mind, body, and spirit. Seeking such a difficult goal is an individual quest and one in which success can only be measured by the individual. Thus all true martial artists derive their sense of self worth from within; they know that no one else can bestow it upon them. Besting another physically cannot add to their own sense of themselves and their accomplishments, and thus they have nothing to prove or gain by fighting. "A person who understands the internal experience of training in the martial arts," says psychologist and martial artist Marc Abrams, "recognizes that you don't have to prove anything. If you are physically attacked, then maybe you'll do something, but until then, your reaction at all times will be to avoid it, because you will be confident of what you can do. And you can create what's called in Japanese, *maai* [proper distance] . . . You have a relationship with your opponent; how are you managing this relationship? It's not a purely physical thing; it's an understanding of the internal. The external will then reflect the internal."

Ultimately, the best martial artist is the one who never gets *into* a fight, for he never loses. It may seem paradoxical, but many martial artists who possess potentially deadly skills are soft-spoken, humble, and friendly people, those whom you would least suspect of possessing such ability. They do not display threatening or aggressive demeanors, but rather exude calm, confidence, and serenity. "The martial arts are about character development, becoming a better person, better skilled, and more human," says tae kwon do master Hee Il Cho. Hanging on the wall in almost every dojo teaching Japanese and Okinawan martial arts is a creed called the *Dojo Kun.* Believed to have been written by Okinawan karate master Shungo "Tode" Sakugawa (1733–1815), these maxims urge us to "Seek perfection of character; be faithful; strive harder; respect others; and refrain from violent behavior." Needless to say, if everyone, not only karate students, lived by this code of conduct, the world would be a better place.

## Martial Arts and Your Child

Whether through friends, school gym classes, advertisements, movies or TV either good or bad, kids today are exposed to the martial arts more than ever before. And regardless whether your child is attracted by the mystique or the reality of martial arts practice, it is very likely that he or she will sooner or later come to you and ask, for example: "Mom, Dad, can I study tae kwon do?" How will you respond?

If you are a typical parent, you will likely be unfamiliar with any specific martial art, and will have to run to the dictionary to look up "tae kwon do," or else ask your child to explain it. And once you find out what it is, your immediate reaction may be fear that your child will get hurt, or even worse, hurt others. Your answer may well be "no."

Although such a response is natural, it is not necessarily wise, for it will have been made without the benefit of factual and relevant information about the martial arts and especially about martial arts for kids. This book is intended to provide that information, to allow you to discuss the martial arts with your child and to make informed decisions about his or her participation. In the course of your reading you will learn many crucial facts, but foremost among them is this: children who study martial arts with the proper guidance will in fact get involved in physical confrontations far less than children who do not study the martial arts. Overall they will be less likely to hurt others, and will be less likely to get hurt. Why?

1) The "aura" of confidence they exude makes them less often chosen as a victim;

2) Confident in their ability to defend themselves, they feel little need, as children often do, to "test" themselves by fighting;

3) Having developed more control over their aggressive instincts, they are better able to defuse situations of potential conflict, as well as better evaluate those situations in which they may truly be in danger.

Part I of this book elaborates on these and other issues. It is our sincere attempt to convince parents that their children should study martial arts, and we discuss the specific physical and mental benefits that may be derived, such as improved motor skills, better self-discipline, reduction of stress levels, and the acquisition of an ability to defend oneself physically. This part concludes with a chapter devoted to the opinions of several members of the medical profession, who attest to these benefits. You will hear from a world-renowned cardiologist, an orthopedic surgeon and team physician for the United States Freestyle Ski Team, three chiropractors, and a pediatrician.

Part II is the real core of the book, presenting information on how to get children involved in a martial art once a decision has been made to participate. The first chapter explains the role and importance of *kata,* or "forms," a fundamental component of most martial arts. This is followed by a discussion of the various martial arts, their characteristics and differences, and how to choose one that is appropriate for your child. The next chapter in this part lists the important questions to ask when deciding on an instructor and school, and gives tips and advice on choosing wisely. The final chapter examines the subject of competition and its role in martial arts training.

Finally, after having heard a great deal from doctors and top martial artists, in Part III we hear from the real "experts," children actively involved in martial arts study, and their families. Although "the ideal situation is when the whole family studies together," says psychologist Steven Handwerker, "this is not essential." What is most important is that the child receives support and encouragement from parents and siblings. Families that respect and show enthusiasm for each other's interests function better as a unit and, at the same time, create strong bonds through caring, sharing, and love.

# PART I

*kung fu*

This general term for Chinese martial arts
simply means "skill" or "ability."

# MOTOR-SKILL DEVELOPMENT

*A Master is one who returns day after day to the basic techniques and fundamentals. Mastery is a matter of daily struggle to perfect the simplest of techniques and ideas.*

—Martial arts axiom

It has been said by yogis that whoever can control the breath can control the mind. The martial arts teach that proper breathing is not only a basic and essential ingredient for maximizing performance in that practice, but is important in all activities in life. In any sport, proper breathing will increase the amount of oxygen in the blood stream and muscles. It allows one to continue to exercise, rather than have to stop due to dizziness or lightheadedness. It also helps the martial artist to properly "explode," breathing out and expending energy as a kick, punch, block, or strike is executed. Proper breathing is essential for the cultivation of *ch'i* (sometimes translated "intrinsic energy"), required to achieve the total unification of the mind and body. Finally, proper breathing is an essential element in stress control.

Knowing how the body moves will promote development of motor skills. The basic stances of the martial arts develop the leg muscles, enabling one to walk and run longer, and to jump higher and farther. Students learn that if they work out of a fundamental horse stance, they can bend the knees in positions that will develop the thigh muscles (quadriceps).

The proper posture required for martial arts will promote a straight and properly aligned spine. It will also give a child better balance as well as better vision (including better peripheral vision). The saying, "Stand tall, walk proud, shoulders back," is often heard in the *dojo* (the martial arts practice area) and is very appropriate. Those who walk and carry themselves properly exude an air of confidence. Children who display such a demeanor are less likely to be picked on by bullies. In short, proper posture has practical physical and mental benefits. The benefits derived by learning proper posture in the dojo can be applied in the schoolyard, the classroom, the home, and in social situations.

## Basic Movements

Most people write and eat with one hand. A right-handed person asked to write with his left hand will probably have a lot of difficulty. The ability to use both hands, feet, and sides of the body equally well is, however, essential to a martial artist. (What good would be the ability to execute a self-defense technique on one's stronger side if an attack comes from the weaker side?) Children initially learn how to put the left leg in front of the right leg, and vice versa, without tripping. This accomplished, they can learn a step-through (a foot maneuver used to attain the same stance but with a different leg forward). Just by executing step-throughs up and down the floor (while incorporating punches, blocks, kicks, strikes, or parries), they are automatically practicing on their right and left sides. Techniques, forms, and sets may initially be practiced on one's stronger side solely for purposes of learning the movements. Once this is accomplished, the other side must be drilled as needed to make it equally effective.

Teaching children how to punch properly is important; punching is taught before blocking, because in order to know how to block a punch, students must first understand the nature of an attack. Before a punch is thrown, the palm faces up in the natural chamber of the fist; as the arm is extended outward to throw the punch, the natural unwinding of the arm muscle will cause the fist to turn palm down. Proper positioning of the fingers is also important, because the thumbs must be protected. Repeating this movement over and over again in a horse stance (without incorporating the additional complexity of foot maneuvers) is a very basic but important component of motor-skill development. The proper torque of the twisting arm, synchronized with the exhalation of the breath, will greatly enhance the speed, snap, and power of the punch. When proficiency is reached, students can begin to execute multiple punches by coordinating the left hand with the right hand (when one hand extends, the other retracts).

Blocking involves movements of ever-increasing complexity. Students need to know what hand should be used, in what direction to block, and how to execute inward, outward, upward, or downward blocks. In blocking, as in punching, the proper alignment of the wrist is essential; a bent wrist can cause injury. So as not to put undue strain on the joints, children are taught how to keep their bones in proper position, and not to overextend their elbows and knees. In all movements, proper body alignment is essential.

Relaxing the shoulders is emphasized, and this is important not only in martial arts, but in other activities as well. Piano students, for example, are told to relax their shoulders; lifting the shoulders increases tension and stress. Relaxed shoulder and back muscles help develop strength, power, and proper posture.

The development of the motor skills of students begins with their very first lesson in martial arts. It is surprising how many children have difficulty stepping through and back without turning their legs inside out or outside in, or crossing their legs up and tripping or falling. Once children become comfortable with properly stepping through and stepping back, they learn to continually be aware of and to enhance their movements through proper body alignment, posture, relaxation, and breathing. To achieve balance with the proper weight distribution, students are taught to place their center of gravity in the mid-section of the body while maintaining level height.

To help them keep their height level, students may be taught to imagine nails sticking out of a ceiling a fraction above their heads. This is one example of another important aspect of training: the development of powers of mental visualization, including the ability to visualize an attack. As part of their training, pilots are now able to simulate on the ground many problem scenarios they might encounter during actual flights (fog, thunderstorms, wind shear, emergency landings). Even though the pilot knows he is actually safe on the ground, he strives to imagine that he is really in the air, where a mistake could lead to catastrophe.

Students of the martial arts should adhere to this philosophy in all aspects of their training. Yes, they can control their punches in the dojo, but they must always imagine that both attack and attacker are real. If they are sloppy, lackadaisical, too gentle, or overly cautious, they will carry this attitude with them into the real world, where it can be dangerous.

Lackadaisical, polite, or "soft" practice does a disservice to both students and their partners. It is better to get a little bruised or hurt in the dojo, than to get seriously hurt on the street. It is also very important to know how an attack and a self-defense technique feel, and to understand what damage would be inflicted if the attack were administered at full force. Such experience can also reduce or eliminate the shock or surprise of a real attack.

In order to deliver more realistic blows to training partners, a variety of protective gear is used, including shin and foot pads, headgear, and mouth guards. Heavy bags, speed bags, and *makiwara* (padded wooden posts for practicing punches and improving concentration) can be used to practice without a partner (while visualizing one). Forms may be practiced without an opponent, but an opponent should always be visualized for maximum effectiveness.

Because new skills learned or new knowledge gained are the building blocks of an inexhaustible storehouse of skill and knowledge, and because all skill and knowledge can be refined and improved upon, children need never become bored; the more they learn, the more they discover there is to learn. Each skill learned increases their confidence, and even though the road keeps getting harder, students will come to believe that just as they have made it to one plateau, hard work will get them to the next. Although the movements become more complex, everything builds on what has been previously learned; therefore, the more solid the foundation, the easier it is to master more complex material. This is why constant practice and refinement of the basics, for novices as well as highly accomplished martial artists, cannot be overemphasized. The grandest skyscraper would collapse if it were built on quicksand.

Many children with seemingly poor coordination have simply never been taught exercises to improve their motor skills. One student, whose parents were distraught because he was labeled "below average" in motor-skill development, after one month in the dojo could do a hundred jumping jacks, and even throw a ball to his teacher while another ball was simultaneously being thrown to him (an exercise to improve eye-hand coordination). It is a shame that children are often negatively labeled when in fact they have simply not been introduced to the proper methods to improve their skills. Even more unfortunately, such children are sometimes led to perform at a low level simply to conform with the opinion of "experts." The child thus labeled was certainly not below average; he even learned how to stand on one leg for a count of ten, then throw a kick. On the first attempt, nine out of ten children cannot do this without falling down.

Failing at something on the first attempt, however, does not indicate a lack of talent or ability. When children are properly taught, in a step-by-step sequence from simple to complex, they can learn to perform most any task. With respect to this particular kicking technique, students are first taught how to relax on one leg by slightly bending the knee, and then to correctly position themselves by breathing properly and finding the center of their bodies. Before students start throwing kicks and executing the follow-up foot maneuvers, however, the teacher makes sure they can hold the one-legged stance for ten seconds, and execute one of the four fundamental kicks (front, back, side, and round-house kick).

After they are able to do this, the teacher will have them execute a foot maneuver by stepping forward or back while adding a kick. At this point, students learn how to develop the kick; they not only kick forward, but snap the kick back (while maintaining their balance), and then step forward. A variation is to bring the leg back, chamber (retract in preparation for kicking), kick, snap back, and step back.

Children taught early on how to develop their motor skills in this way will gain a better understanding of how the body moves and functions, and will likely do better in every other physical activity they undertake. And, of course, improved motor skills will enhance their performance of self-defense techniques.

## Sets and Forms

Sets and forms are movements of greater complexity that help develop coordination and are used in many martial-arts systems. Sets are exercises focusing on specific skills, actions, or parts of the body—stances, kicks, finger strikes, etc. In kenpo, an American karate system, there are striking sets, kicking sets, blocking sets, stance sets, an elbow set, and coordination sets. We can also take sets and make additional coordination exercises out of them. The basic kenpo blocking set, for example, can be practiced with one hand performing an upward, inward, outward, downward, elbow, and push-down block, while the other hand performs the identical routine backwards. This exercise has been successfully utilized with handicapped children.

Forms, also called by the Japanese and Okinawan term *kata,* incorporate various strikes, kicks, blocks, stances, and foot maneuvers into a choreographed routine. Although forms can be practiced with training partners, they are designed to be beneficial when practicing alone. Again, students should keep in mind the purpose of the form, and imagine actual opponents.

### Self-Defense Techniques

Motor-skill development is put to full use in practicing self-defense techniques. Coordination, including eye-hand coordination, balance, ambidextrous development, and foot maneuvering are all utilized.

In all martial arts, balance is essential both for good leverage and to attain the position from which one can most effectively thwart an attack and execute a self-defense technique. When kicking, one or both legs are off the ground. If balance is not maintained, kicks are much less effective. The benefits gained from acquiring good balance can also carry over into everyday life. People with good balance are less likely to fall if they are not holding onto a strap or pole in a suddenly lurching or stopping subway car or bus. They will be more likely to stay on their feet and avoid injury if they slip on a wet surface.

Checking, sometimes called trapping, is utilized in many martial arts systems. Most of the time, checking is synchronized with a strike. When one hand strikes or blocks, the other will check (sometimes pinning or pulling). Coordination is therefore necessary for the harmonious marriage of all movements. Bag work is one means by which eye-hand coordination can be developed. The ability to coordinate what the eye sees with what the hands do is important to all martial artists. While hitting the speed bag and double-ended striking bag, for example, timing, focus, balance, leverage, and speed are all improved.

Forms (as well as sets and self-defense techniques) should be executed very slowly at first. Not only will the form then be developed properly, but the added concentration on each detail will improve balance, movement, and breath control. An analogy can be made to a pianist working on a difficult passage with a metronome. He will start at an extremely slow tempo, because in many respects it is more difficult to play slowly than it is to play quickly. With each repetition, the metronome will be set to the next higher speed. The pianist gradually works his way up to a fast tempo. In the meantime, his control of the passage is increased, because he has played the passage in many tempos; his muscular memory is also increased by the constant repetition.

Each form focuses on a specific area of study; the *sanchin* kata (in the *goju-ryu* system) and the *hangetsu* kata (in the shotokan system) are forms which help students control their breathing. Some are practiced to develop speed; others are used to develop strength; some focus on a combination of skills. Sets and forms increase in difficulty and complexity to conform to a student's current level of proficiency, but even proficient martial artists should always continue to practice the fundamental sets and forms, in addition to always practicing and refining their basic components. As stated previously, students may initially practice techniques, forms, and sets on their strong side solely for purposes of learning the movements. Once the knowledge of the movements is acquired, however, they should be practiced on the weaker side until it is equally effective.

When a set, form, or self-defense technique is mastered, it should be performed on as many surfaces as possible. One cannot choose the surface or environment where an actual attack will occur; he must be ready for all contingencies. Someone may have become proficient in a self-defense technique in the dojo, but be thrown for a loop if attacked on ice, where maintaining balance will be critical and difficult. In water, there will be added resistance; sand does not offer a hard surface for support, while a hill lacks the level surface one may be used to in the dojo. A fight may go to the ground, but unless a martial artist's system specializes in fighting from such a position, staying on the feet is preferable. How a person maneuvers his feet often determines the outcome of a confrontation. How effective would the world's hardest puncher be if he were off-balance, or if his punch was not synchronized with his feet?

Although improving breathing, posture, balance, coordination, and strength, as well as mental visualization skills and ambidextrous capabilities are critically important to the successful growth and development of children, many children do not participate in activities designed to promote those goals. A good martial arts training program provides such activities. Moreover, the training need not be onerous or boring. A good martial arts instructor will make them  seem like a game, and students who are having fun will want to continue their training; they will not have to be forced. And because people tend to excel at what they enjoy, they will continue to improve.

# SELF-DISCIPLINE

*Children confident in their physical and mental abilities feel no need to prove anything via aggressive or obnoxious behavior. The mental discipline of the martial arts, coupled with strenuous physical activity, is a perfect formula for raising children.*

—Cheryl Wheeler, C.N.
world kickboxing champion

No matter what style or system parents choose for their children, a true martial arts school will foster self-discipline. Children learn that they cannot always have what they want, when they want it, simply because they want it. They also learn that martial arts proficiency does not come overnight, and the only way to achieve it is through diligent and systematic practice over a period of years.

In the martial arts dojo, children learn the virtue of patience in a non-competitive atmosphere. Characterizing the dojo as "non-competitive" may come as a surprise to those whose conception of martial arts is derived from popular media portrayals, in which good guys and bad guys are forever having it out. In fact, however, it is stressed in the dojo that one is only in competition with one's self, and that focusing on someone else's relative rate of advancement is irrelevant and counterproductive. The only thing relevant is that students continue to learn and improve their skills, no matter how slow the progress appears to be. It does not matter how long it takes to get to the destination, only that progress is made toward it.

With this in mind, children will achieve greater results in a shorter amount of time if they discipline themselves to focus on the task at hand, rather than on larger future goals. A yellow-belt student learning a self-defense technique or a form, and thinking about the other techniques and forms required for an orange belt (or worrying about how many years it will take him to get a black belt), is not addressing his task at hand with full focus and concentration.

The discipline it takes for children to stick it out in an intricate art that does not promise instant rewards can only carry over into and enhance the possibilities for success in many other aspects of their lives, such as schoolwork. They will learn to budget their time, and will come to realize that the same discipline that enabled them to improve in martial arts and advance to higher belt rankings can be applied to schoolwork, with similar results. The martial arts foster the attitude, "If you want something, you must work for it" and further demonstrates that if you work hard for it, you can get it.

The dojo is a kind of sanctuary, a place where the problems and worries of the day should be left outside the door, and where full concentration should be utilized. Before entering the training area, students take off their shoes and bow, a gesture of respect for the school and the art. Instructors are addressed as "Sensei, " "Sifu," "Sir," or other appropriate titles out of respect for their greater knowledge. Respect for the dojo is also maintained by refraining from eating, drinking, or smoking there, and by keeping it clean. Maintaining a clean, well-groomed body with manicured nails and a clean *gi* (uniform) shows respect for peers, instructors, the dojo, the martial art, and the students themselves. No profanity is allowed, and no horseplay is tolerated. Time spent at the dojo should be enjoyable, but it is for serious training only.

Is military-style discipline good for a child? "We don't run our school militaristically," said Kathy Owen, a fifth-degree black belt in kenpo. "Little kids can't discern the difference between someone just yelling at them, or doing it for 'motivational' purposes. They don't interpret it as motivational, as an adult can."

Ms. Owen goes on to mention that medical doctors, including psychiatrists and psychologists, are recommending that children diagnosed with ADD (attention deficit disorder) enroll in martial arts schools because it teaches them control. ADD children are typically unable to control their responses to external stimuli; often they cannot sit still or control what they say. Because of these symptoms, there are often learning disabilities associated with this condition and many children suffering from ADD take regular medication.

Dr. Marc Abrams, a psychologist, recommends martial arts as a good adjunct to behavioral therapy and medication. Dr. Steven Handwerker, also a psychologist, believes martial arts can be helpful, but only if approached with the proper philosophy. He feels that if study is undertaken merely for purposes of physical competition or achievement, it would not be beneficial for children with this problem. "In order to be effective," he said, "martial arts must be practiced with a focus on the mental, spiritual, emotional, and physical aspects."

Are there significant differences between ADD and ADHD (attention deficit hyperactivity disorder)? "There are many different theories," says Dr. Handwerker, "but I believe that there is a correlation between ADD and ADHD. More important than labeling children, however, is that they feel viable and valid; children must feel that they can accomplish something. If such children are in a situation in which they feel overwhelmed, they can develop even stronger feelings of insecurity and self-hatred (one of the interactive components of ADD). That's very important; they must feel competent. One of the causes of ADD on an emotional level is a lack of nurturing instruction. The ideal situation, and not just for kids who have ADD, is for the whole family to study together. As long as the children and the parents aren't being competitive, this is one of the healthiest activities in which a family can participate."

As mentioned earlier, children often "live down" to the labels placed on them, rather than transcending such artificial boundaries and achieving what they are really capable of. "I try not to label kids," said Dr. Handwerker. "Once a doctor labels a child, the parents follow suit; it then gets passed down to the kid, who now is expected to perform according to the parameters of his diagnosis."

Can a poor diet exacerbate a condition such as ADD? "Definitely," says Dr. Handwerker. "Kids who live on sugar and junk food make their problem worse than it already is. I feel that diet is something that should be discussed by the instructor; it's part of the discipline of the martial arts."

Martial arts involves meditation and concentration, so children will improve their ability to concentrate and to apply theoretical concepts along practical and physical avenues. "They will feel more secure in the knowledge of what they can do," said Dr. Handwerker. "Martial arts study builds a sense of independence, because the children are actually doing and achieving something for themselves. With a proper attitude and attention span, children can start as young as four or five years old. My daughter started at the age of five, and loved it from the start.

"Martial arts do not merely involve abstract memorization, as if memorizing answers for a test. Because you're memorizing and internalizing techniques that can save your life someday, there's a depth to the memorization and understanding (created through concentration). As they develop their *ch'i,* concentration, practical physical memory in the body, and application of their techniques, they will discover that their mind actually becomes stronger. In all the advanced systems of the martial arts, the mind is more powerful than the body. In other words, the mind activates the *ch'i* that moves the body, so the mind is always first."

In summary, the martial arts provide a marvelous opportunity to instill self-discipline, confidence, and control in children, even those who are naturally unruly or who suffer from conditions that make appropriate behavior difficult for them. Still, "parents should understand" says eighth-degree black belt and kenpo instructor Gilbert Velez, "that we're not psychologists, doctors, or therapists. The parents should be the real teachers. We have their children only one or two hours a week; the parents have them the rest of the time." He feels, as we do, that the younger a child starts on a regular program of martial arts training (age three and a half or four, for example), the better.

Speaking of his system (but a description which applies to other systems), Mr. Velez says that kenpo is very much an individual pursuit. Even if a child has not mastered all the self-defense techniques for his belt level, "if I see a student making progress, I'll promote him. What's important is that he does his *forms* well." He completely agrees with the expression, "Talent is ninety-eight percent perspiration and two percent inspiration." Velez was an art major in college, and in addition to being a kenpo instructor is an accomplished mariachi musician. When he was in college, he remembers observing some "untalented" art and music majors and asking himself, "What are they doing here?" But they worked hard, and ended up surpassing the supposedly talented students. In other words, talent can be acquired . . . and talent combined with hard work is what is often called genius.

# STRESS REDUCTION

*When there is no more conflict in your mind, then you are really living. This is the true gift karate can give us.*

—Teruyuki Okazaki
chairman and chief instructor
International Shotokan Karate Federation
1982 Man of the Year, *Black Belt* Hall of Fame

Stress, defined as emotional or intellectual tension, is widely prevalent in today's society, especially in big cities. While a certain amount of stress is perfectly normal, it has been shown that large amounts of continuous stress can lead to such maladies as heart attacks, ulcers, and even the breakdown of the immune system. Stress encompasses many areas of life: a businessman can become "stressed out," because he allows himself to believe that every deal he is working on is a life or death situation; a student may be stressed out from studying, and worrying whether or not he will pass an important exam or be accepted by a particular university; a parent can become stressed out from a house full of screaming kids. Situations such as traffic jams, crowded subway cars, and noise can bring stress about or exacerbate it.

Inherent in stress is worry: "Will I succeed at this task?" "Will someone else beat me to a goal?" "Will the other guy get the promotion even though my production was equal to his?" Such worries are often "other-directed" rather than "self-directed," likely resulting from our modern competitive life-styles.

Training in martial arts can play a significant role in the reduction of stress, a fact concurred with by experts such as Dr. Stanley Katz, chief cardiologist at North Shore University Hospital in Manhasset, New York. Dr. Ellen Sandler, a chiropractor and martial artist, says that "training teaches people to control and release their emotions, which relates to the level of stress. You wouldn't necessarily call it 'stress' when referring to four-year-olds, because they don't think in those terms. But they *do* get very worked up with their emotions, and martial arts gives them a positive outlet."

Because the dojo is a place to leave one's troubles outside the door, it is the perfect environment in which to "release" stress, through concentrating while hitting the bag, performing sparring drills, engaging in freestyle sparring, or performing any number of physical activities. Students will in most cases be calmer, and less stressed out when they leave the dojo. Subsequently, they will be able to perform better in school, business, and life in general. Dr. Katz believes, moreover, that one can deal with adverse situations, such as confrontations with school bullies, if one is calm and relaxed. Children further find that the time taken to train at the dojo and practice at home does not negatively affect their schoolwork. On the contrary, being presented with a task requiring complex skills, and mastering them, gives them the confidence that they can achieve equally rewarding results with their schoolwork if they budget their time properly and apply an equivalent amount of discipline.

I recall driving with a highly stressed out person in the car, who would launch into an obscenity-laced tirade whenever an oncoming motorist took too long to make a left turn and held us up, or a car ahead did not instantly move when the light turned green. He told me later that on his doctor's orders he had given up his license. His blood pressure was very high, and he said that he would have probably had a heart attack by now had he continued to drive. Such a person would be an ideal candidate for a "before and after" study of what martial arts training can do. We are not suggesting that martial arts training offers a complete cure—only that it has the potential to enormously reduce stress.

The dojo, as mentioned, is a place to leave all boyfriend or girlfriend, marital, financial, and personal problems outside the door. Proper martial arts instruction will show that negative thoughts simply interfere with concentration and thus hinder training; conversely, developing and applying the necessary focus and concentration, as children will be taught in the dojo, helps reduce the power of those external concerns.

Hard practice provides a respite from the troubles of the outside world. Being in class is simply about the individual student and his or her practice, with no thought given to how he or she may look to other students. When class is in progress, one doesn't turn around to see who has arrived late; it doesn't matter. It has been said of basketball great Larry Bird that when he was shooting, the building could have been tumbling down around him and it wouldn't have made any difference. Nothing but the ball and the hoop existed. This is the kind of concentration and focus that students of the martial arts aspire to, and these can be applied in the outside world to reduce the effects of stress.

Another lesson children will learn is that worry, a chief component  of stress, is nothing more than fear arising from an often unwarranted assumption that something will not turn out the way they want it to. Worry is a wasteful emotion, because often more time is spent worrying about an impending event than taking constructive action to bring about a desired result.

What a child is taught about failure very often plays a major role in his confidence and performance. So many of the great pioneers, inventors, business people, and sports stars failed many times before they became successful. Thomas Edison tried thousands of filament materials before his first successful light bulb was invented. Babe Ruth was a strike-out king as well as a home-run king. The salesman who knocks on a thousand doors to make one sale is more successful than one who knocks on only ten doors but makes no sale, even though the former experiences failure 989 more times than the latter.

Indeed, the degree of success is often proportional to the number of times one fails. An intelligent person learns from his failures as well as his successes, and thus is not afraid to fail. He knows that the seeds of success lie in failure. The karate student who loses a match is taught to analyze precisely what he did wrong, so that it is less likely to happen again, at least not in the same way. The pain can even be seen as "positive" in the sense that it gives the student first-hand experience of what can happen if he doesn't block or dodge a punch.

The same can be said in business or other everyday situations. In *Winning Through Intimidation,* Robert Ringer writes that whenever he was victimized by someone in the business world, rather than being immobilized by feelings of hatred or revenge, he would transpose the source of his difficulty to within, where it belonged. He even felt that he owed the perpetrator of the wrong a debt of gratitude for teaching him a lesson. That person he now regarded as another professor at "The School of Hard Knocks," and if he lost thousands of dollars, this was viewed as tuition for the course.

Students of martial arts are taught that when learning a self-defense technique, a form, or anything intricate or complicated, they must allow themselves to fail. They are shown that failing is inherent in practice, and they are exhorted to try and try again. Soon they begin to discover what works and what does not work; they learn to experiment, to mold, to evolve, and eventually to achieve proficiency. Then they practice even more to retain what they have learned. Experiencing this process of growth demonstrates to them a clear path for overcoming obstacles, not only in the dojo but elsewhere in life. And gaining confidence in one's ability to overcome obstacles is the best way to eliminate worry and the stress that it creates.

# SELF-DEFENSE

*If you're really interested in self-defense, then you need to train specifically for that. Because when you get hit you can't stop to think. All you can do is react, and you will react however you trained.*

—Professor Wally Jay
founder of Small Circle Jujitsu

We all recognize that life is full of dangers and we all take reasonable steps to insure ourselves against accidents and disasters. We have insurance if we drive an automobile, we buy mortgage insurance and homeowner's insurance to protect our property and we pay into pension plans and social security to ensure we are well-off financially when we reach old age. We spend hundreds of dollars on alarm systems for our cars, homes, and businesses, but somehow, most of us neglect to insure adequately our most important asset—the personal safety of ourselves and our loved ones.

As much as we would like not to believe it, we are living in violent times. One need only pick up a newspaper or turn on the news to hear of the latest murder or other serious crime. Some people carry mace for protection, but if a sudden attack occurs, there may be no time to use it. Others opt for guns, but a concealed weapon is illegal in most states and statistics on shooting accidents have shown that guns can be as dangerous to the innocent as they are to the criminal.

Courses are offered that teach common-sense safety precautions: walk in lighted areas; check the back seat of your car before getting into it; don't enter an elevator with a suspicious looking person in it; avoid using automatic-teller machines at night; and ride in the subway car with the conductor. Other courses teach physical responses to attacks using ordinary objects such as keys, books, hairbrushes, bags, pencils, or nail files as defensive weapons. School children can even be taught how to use these items, as well as their books and bags. However, a victim may not have time to grasp the needed item, or may be incapacitated by a sudden attack. In a dangerous world, the best way to tip the scales in your favor is to be trained in a comprehensive self-defense system.

We are not suggesting that a physical counterattack is always necessary; martial arts training can help ward off or deflect danger in a number of ways. Students of the martial arts tend to walk with poise and purpose, for example, which experts advise is a good way to avoid becoming a criminal target. Muggers are looking for easy "targets of opportunity," and will think twice about attacking anyone walking tall and proud, even if the person is not imposing physically. Someone who is slouching and looking down will not likely be physically and mentally able to react as quickly, and thus appears to be easier prey.

Moreover, proficient martial artists are better able to sense, and thus avoid, potential altercations. Children trained in the martial arts will be able to spot aggressive children in a schoolyard and avoid getting into confrontational situations. Walking in the street, they'll be able to sense that someone is acting aggressively. They will put themselves out of harm's way, and subsequently eliminate the possibility of getting into a fight.

Next to avoiding a fight altogether, the most important rule of self-defense is simply to get out of the way. One cannot strike someone who isn't there. Students of the martial arts are taught how to move defensively, simultaneously executing clearing or blocking motions. At higher levels, they are taught to get out of the way just by maneuvering the body. As this is done, they learn to breathe properly and to maintain balance.

When working out in the dojo, students are exhorted to treat their sparring bouts as if they were real-life situations of potential danger. With this attitude, it is easier for them to put out a hundred percent. Their mental acuity is heightened, and the blood and *ch'i* begin to pump. They are taught how to snap into that same level of intensity if a dangerous situation should arise on the street. That is what mental discipline is all about.

In class, however, the training focuses on movement and technique, so no one gets hurt. In fact, proper training helps students control and direct their intensity. Except in special circumstances, students do not strike training partners with full force in the dojo, although they could easily do so if they wished. As the late kenpo senior grand master Ed Parker said, "I don't teach students how to pull a punch; I teach them how to *control* a punch."

The martial arts teach children to be humble and at peace with themselves; it is then easier to be at peace with others. They are encouraged to be assertive, but not aggressive. An assertive person exudes confidence by the way he carries himself. He gets his point across in a positive way without bullying. Parents will have peace of mind knowing that their children, properly instructed in martial arts, will never be the ones to initiate force. Their knowledge and skills will give them the necessary self-esteem to walk away from a fight without feeling like a coward. They will use their martial arts skills only as a last resort. The more proficient they become, the more self-control they acquire. And ultimately they will come to realize that the best fighter never gets into a fight, and therefore never loses. The knowledge that they can defend themselves will also make them more confident, and this confidence will carry over into all areas of their lives. They will send out the "vibes" of confidence and self-assurance. A positive attitude is the result of feeling good about oneself, and the child who does cannot easily be intimidated.

Moreover, "self-defense" relates to a broader realm than simply the ability to oppose a physical attack. Those who are well-trained in the martial arts are better able to respond in crisis situations. They are able to "keep their cool," to focus and to concentrate in emergencies. Because they are in good shape physically, they have the strength and stamina to aid others in distress. Their better balance and coordination makes them better able to avoid or to sustain accidents such as slips, falls, or blows without serious injury. Finally, looking at the broadest interpretation of "self-defense," we can include the general ability to ward off illness that comes with good health.

# THE DOCTORS SPEAK

*The real secrets within martial arts are speed, power, flexibility, and endurance, and how to achieve these and how to employ them. We are particularly concerned that our actions benefit the heart/mind and bring nourishment to the spirit. This is not simply a sport; this is life itself.*

—Lu Xiaoling
U.S. coach, 1993 and 1995 World Wu Shu Championships
gold medalist, International Martial Arts Championships, 1989

We've discussed many specific benefits that children, or anyone, can derive from the practice of a martial art. In this chapter we will present the opinions of medical professionals on martial arts study in the context of general physical fitness. The martial arts are, indeed, great for attaining and maintaining physical well-being.

Fitness plays an important role not only in the prevention of heart disease, but in preventing recurrences of serious events for those who already have heart disease. "I'm a firm believer in physical fitness," says Dr. Stanley Katz, a cardiologist, "not only as beneficial in avoiding cardiac disease, but *all* diseases." He believes that having a healthy body is an important prerequisite to having a healthy mind; they should go hand in hand.

Many sports and activities can provide us with a great cardiovascular workout, but not all of them require complete concentration. Running, for example, is a great form of exercise, but most people run on "automatic pilot," thinking about unrelated things. Martial arts, on the other hand, is exercise that is completely controlled by the mind. "You have to think all the time," says Dr. Katz, "so it requires a lot more mental discipline than most other physical activities; if you train in karate for an hour, you have to think about it for an hour, so your mind and body are coordinated during this time."

Are the hearts of most kids healthy enough for them to safely participate in martial arts or other sports and physical activities? "Most emphatically, yes," says Dr. Katz. "If a child has a heart murmur, however, a pediatrician would pick this up during an examination. It would then be important for a pediatric cardiologist to discover where it's coming from, in order to determine if it's safe for him to participate in competitive sports."

Do our hearts actually become stronger through cardiovascular activity? "Let me clarify a few things," says Dr. Katz. "When you train in karate or other activities and become physically fit, it's not the heart that becomes fit. An average person [who trains regularly] will have a lower resting heart rate, in the sixty to eighty range, than less physically active people; an Olympic athlete would be in the forty-five to fifty range. But it's the body, not the heart, that's fit. Because the body is fit, it's requiring less oxygen, so the heart has to pump less blood to the body, and that's why the heart rate goes down. It's not that the heart becomes stronger; it's just that the body and all your muscles are functioning more efficiently, and therefore requiring less oxygen. As a result, the heart doesn't have to pump out as much blood, and the heartbeat goes down."

If done wisely, any kind of exercise is great. We can be tired and sweaty after a vigorous workout, but it's not a lethargic kind of tiredness; we feel exhilarated. Dr. Katz concurs: "People talk about an exercise high," he says. "When you exercise, you release substances in your body called endorphins. They act like morphine; they're a morphine derivative, and they make you feel good . . . I'm a regular jogger, and when I skip my usual routine, I don't have the same drive and energy."

Dr. Robert Schwartz is an orthopedic surgeon. The majority of his practice deals with sports-related injuries, with a focus on knees and shoulders. Since 1985, he has been the team physician for the U.S. Merchant Marine Academy Football Team at Kings Point, New York, and since 1992 a team physician for the U.S. Freestyle Ski Team. "Professionally," he says, "I think the martial arts are an excellent individual developmental activity that enables children to gain a variety of benefits all at the same time. Regarding the mind, martial arts teach discipline, respect, and control. In the 'physical' realm, martial arts improve flexibility, and foster a coordinated mind and body control, which is similar to dance in many ways."

Dr. Schwartz believes that in order to prevent injuries in a variety of different sporting activities, it's important for a growing child to have good flexibility. "It's not uncommon," he said, "to see kids who haven't developed the flexibility of their musculo-skeletal system. Problems with recurring tendonitis, or muscle strains of the hamstrings and calf are a result of this poor flexibility. I feel that the very sedentary nature of a lot of children's activities contribute to this. When they do get into sports, most of them will focus on the sporting activities, rather than on the conditioning and strength-related developmental processes that are necessary to really bring them up into the sport."

Dr. Schwartz encounters far fewer martial arts-related injuries in children than in adults. The schools he has observed generally provide a safe environment; the kids utilize appropriate protective devices, and classes are usually conducted on matted surfaces to protect them during throws and falls. Contact does not play a major role in the beginning stages of their training.

Does he find that there are more injuries in contact sports, such as football, lacrosse, soccer, and basketball than in martial arts? "Yes," he said. "I look at martial arts as similar to a ladder or staircase, where certain skills require a particular level of mastery. Until you've mastered those skills, you're not allowed to proceed to the next level of performance. In many of the other activities, however, that staircase effect isn't as well delineated. It's also not uncommon to see a lot of size mismatches; a small seventh grader, for example, might be matched up against a very large seventh grader, who outweighs him by fifty pounds, in a football game. That's quite a big disparity, and in such situations, the potential for injury is increased."

Dr. Schwartz says that because of their unique process of growth, kids have more of a propensity towards fractures than injuries to the ligaments. This holds true until children reach their mid teens. At this time, the bones become more mineralized, and stronger than the ligaments, which are then more prone to injury. Children up to about age fourteen more commonly suffer fractures of the wrist, elbow, and lower leg, above the ankle, than they do fractures of or around the knee. It would take quite a lot of trauma to injure this area, where the bones are actually weaker than the soft tissue support structures for the joints.

Sometimes we hear that holding stances too long are bad for the knees, or too much kicking will strain the joints. Are these fallacies? Dr. Schwartz believes so, and would have no great concerns regarding a child's propensity for injury in a martial arts class. He believes they have less of a chance of being injured there than in many other activities.

"Martial arts, dance, and gymnastics are three activities that probably give you the most significant total body training. The problem with gymnastics, and maybe to a lesser extent with dance, is that there is a tendency toward overusing certain movements. Dancers and gymnasts occasionally develop stress fractures, but I can't say I've ever encountered this in a martial arts practitioner."

Dr. Daniel L. Krauz is not only a chiropractor, but a black belt in judo, and has extensive high school and college wrestling experience. He believes that studying a martial art is a great way to develop posture and balance, and when you teach children these two things, "you're teaching them the essentials for a healthy life." The more balanced your body is, the less friction will be created on the joints, and consequently, there will be less wear and tear. Like Dr. Schwartz, he places great emphasis on flexibility. "If flexibility is developed at a young age," he says, "you'll have more of an edge when you're older, and you'll be less prone to arthritic changes, what we call osteoarthritis, or wear and tear on the joints. We're all going to develop osteoarthritis, but you'll find senseis who are seventy years old and still very flexible. If your posture and flexibility is very good, your body's efficiency will be at its highest level, and you'll have better balance. The better your balance, the greater your capacity for power. When you have all three, the full potential of your body can be realized."

Another benefit of martial arts training, discussed earlier, is that it develops both sides of the body, as well as ambidexterity, something that most other sports do not. A right-handed person will almost always throw a baseball with his right hand, for example. Similarly, in sports such as basketball and football, we usually dribble, shoot, and throw with our dominant hand.

Dr. Ellen Sandler, a chiropractor with a background in martial arts and dance, says that martial arts have been found to be beneficial to children suffering from dyslexia. This neurological "switching" in the brain causes a person to mix up the right and left sides. The correction of this problem is greatly aided by an effort to use both sides equally, as well as by engaging in activities that require opposite feet and arms to work in conjunction. These so-called "cross/crawl" patterns are very common in the martial arts (where they are referred to as "push-pull" movements), and although they will not necessarily cure dyslexic children, their emphasis on coordinating right and left, as well as forward and back movement helps reinforce other therapies the children may be undergoing.

Wouldn't gymnastics or dance be just as beneficial? "Martial arts tends to provide more structure for young children," said Dr. Sandler. "Children who get into dance are primarily doing creative movement at the beginning; linear and repetitive movement is not stressed. There is some emphasis placed on developing the right and left sides, but in a more musical and creative way. Ballet develops wonderful posture, but it's not spinally correct. The chest is jutted forward a little bit too much, you're arching your back, and you're opening up your hips in an unnatural way. I love dance, but from a professional point of view, ballet dancers, and to some extent even modern dancers, are fighting the natural structure of the body. Martial arts, on the other hand, are structurally compatible with the body. Gymnastics enhances flexibility and coordination, but as in ballet, you're exaggerating the posture. When you're involved in martial arts, you're learning a certain level of repetitive, structured discipline that the other activities don't have. In addition, the posture that we develop through our martial arts training is very friendly to the spine. In everyday life, people tend to lock their knees and jut their pelvis forward. This sets the pelvis and the rest of the spine out of alignment. When you concentrate on keeping your body erect, with your head squarely on your shoulders, the hips slightly tucked under, and the knees slightly bent, you're learning how to carry yourself properly. Consequently, your muscles are being used in a very positive way."

Dr. Stanley Weindorf, a pediatrician, says that he very rarely sees sports injuries in the age group of four to ten. "Young kids," he said, "have not yet acquired enough size and weight to pose a significant threat of injury to their peers. The largest growth spurt usually starts at approximately age twelve. Injuries are more common at this time, because a larger child will generate more force; more force results in more injuries. In addition, the level of competition starts to increase."

Dr. Weindorf also stressed that performing a sport or physical activity with poor mechanics increases the child's tendency to sustain injuries such as strains and sprains. Good martial arts teachers stress proper stretching at the beginning of classes, to minimize injuries. In addition, most systems are structured by means of colored belts. This hierarchy helps insure that the child proceeds with his training in a gradual but steady manner. Each bit of knowledge builds on previous knowledge; each skill builds on, and reinforces previously acquired skills. A beginning student could not be expected to master advanced movements before first assimilating his fundamentals. This is why sparring, for example, is not recommended for a beginning student.

The possibility of injury does exist, as in all sports and physical activities, but with intelligent precautions, the risks are greatly minimized. Dr. Weindorf has a nephew who holds a black belt in karate, so he was able to observe the benefits of studying a martial art, from a developmental and medical perspective, first-hand. "What they emphasized," he says, "was control: control of your limbs and your body, so that you could really make it do what you wanted. He was then able to apply this ability to any other sport he participated in, whether it was soccer, swimming, baseball, or football. The study of martial arts taught him a lot from a mental as well as physical aspect."

"I think sports are great," said Dr. Weindorf. "Martial arts, in particular, teaches kids that there is an appropriate action for an appropriate situation, whether it be how you treat an adult, how you treat your friends, or how you react in a challenging situation. You can almost always tell when a child has trained in a martial art. Although they're confident, and walk tall and proud, they're respectful, peaceful, and avoid physical confrontations at all costs. Another great benefit, is that the discipline necessary to master a martial art almost always carries over into their schoolwork."

Dr. Roger Russell is not only a chiropractic orthopedist, but a fifth-degree black belt in kenpo. In fact, he put himself through college, graduate school, and postgraduate school by running karate schools. He believes that martial arts promote flexibility, one of its most important benefits from a physical standpoint. "If you have flexibility," says Dr. Russell, "you will reduce the number of injuries you have, such as groin strains, by a significant amount. In martial arts, you're taught from day one how to stretch properly. This not only helps a child achieve greater flexibility; it helps them to maintain it. In addition, the eye-hand coordination and dexterity that one develops spills over into any other sport they participate in."

When we practice a martial art, we are continuously kicking, twisting, and turning the body. Can this be injurious to the spine, knees, and hips? "First of all," says Dr. Russell, "if you have a teacher who teaches you how to punch and kick correctly, you're not going to have strain or stress on the joints. Secondly, joints rely on movement for their nutrition. They are avascular—

lacking a blood supply—and rely on synovial fluid—the fluid inside the cavity of the joints—which bathes the joint surfaces as you move. This is what gives joints their nutrition, so all joints rely on movement. It's interesting that one of the only set of joints that don't develop osteoarthritis are the ribs, because we're always breathing, so there's always movement occurring in those joints. When joints do not move, that's when they tighten up on you, particularly when you're older. Joints are not going to tighten up when you're an adolescent, but if they don't get the movement they need, they can tighten up when you're forty, fifty, or sixty years old. The cartilage starts to wear and break down, because it's not getting the nutrition it needs, and the body comes in with its cement—calcium—and starts laying that down to help stiffen that area up even more, so you get a vicious cycle."

"Motion, therefore, should be maintained in all the joints, and studying martial arts is a great way to achieve this. It goes without saying, that if children perform splits or kicks incorrectly, they may risk subjecting themselves to injury. A competent instructor, however can teach children the proper way to execute these movements." As in other sports and activities, martial artists are not immune to occasional bumps and bruises. But the use of padding, combined with a good instructor, one who emphasizes control, makes the study of a martial art a safe and enjoyable activity.

# PART II

*judo*

The characters for this popular
Japanese martial art literally mean
the "gentle way."

# THE ESSENCE OF KATA

*The samurai used kata for meditation. The true
meaning and value of the kata have been lost in
most martial arts schools. In fact, the ignorant
have degraded it as classical deadwood. You
will note that those who do not know the value
and true purpose of kata always espouse the
need for physical excellence, without realizing
that the true fight is with life itself. The man
who conquers himself can easily conquer the
outside, because then no obstacle is too great.*

—Richard Kim, Ph.D.
1973 Instructor of the Year, *Black Belt* Hall of Fame
1986 Man of the Year, *Black Belt* Hall of Fame

Ed Parker defined a form, or kata, as: "a short story of
motion. It consists of basic movements of offense and
defense incorporated into a dance-like routine for purposes of exercising, training without a partner, or training at home. It is an index of movements that gives specific answers, as well as speculative interpretations to
combat situations." Katas provide structured movements through which to execute the technical compo-

nents of a martial art. When practicing forms, students strive to maintain proper body alignment, straight wrists, and correct positioning of the fists. They learn how to focus, how to perform movements on the right and left sides, and how to move in different directions.

It is important for children to be able to maneuver and still keep good balance by centering the body, and kata practice provides a perfect vehicle for the development and utilization of these and other motor skills. Moreover, the constant repetition necessary to perfect a newly learned kata does wonders for a child's self-discipline. We find that concentrating is one of the hardest tasks for children and the practice of kata is a wonderful way for developing this. Putting structure in their lives helps children in everything they do. For this reason, many medical professionals, as mentioned in the chapter "Self-Discipline," believe the study of kata, and martial arts in general, to be beneficial for children with ADD (attention deficit disorder) and ADHD (attention deficit hyperactivity disorder). Because practicing kicks, punches, strikes, and blocks can become boring after awhile, good instructors change things around by isolating and concentrating on different combinations of specific movements; by making games of practice, children will have fun and want to learn. Through kata study students are able to practice all the basic strikes, blocks, and kicks in meaningful choreographed movements.

Sometimes sets—training drills for specific skill areas, such as stances, blocks, kicks—are first taught, after which the instructor combines elements of those sets into the more complex katas. It is impossible to learn katas just by seeing them and going through the motions; you have to feel them. Katas develop excellent visualization skills, so that those who are proficient in kata feel as if they are applying actual self-defense moves. (The Japanese refer to the application of kata as *bunkai*).

Historically, katas have been utilized to disguise the self-defense or fighting applications of the movements when the practice of martial arts was not allowed. For example, the early Brazilian *capoeira* stylists camouflaged such applications in dance movements accompanied by music. Similarly, when the Spaniards conquered the Philippines and forbade the natives to use their swords and knives, "The Filipinos," writes Abon "Garimot" Baet in the April 1997 issue of *Inside Kung-fu,* "developed the *moro-moro,* a socio-religious play designed to surreptitiously incorporate the fighting techniques of *kali* into its creative dances and movements." Bamboo sticks were utilized in these plays.

Some martial arts systems, such as the Philippine art *kali* and Bruce Lee's jeet kune do, claim they do not use katas, but they do utilize various sets for practicing techniques; most systems, however, such as traditional judo do employ actual katas. The shotokan karate system has five basic *heihan* ("peaceful mind") katas; practicing these every day will supposedly make one a calmer and more mentally well-balanced person. T'ai chi ch'uan utilizes slow, graceful, and fluid katas, as if the student were appearing in a slow-motion film or performing mime. But the movements help to develop power and *ch'i* (*ki* in Japanese). Karate and kung fu masters say that the development of *ch'i* promotes health, increased energy, and improved fluidity of movement.

With further practice, katas help to "fuse" together physical and mental development. Thought and action become less distinct. Kata practice can in fact be thought of as representative of the spiritual side of martial arts; dedicated practitioners work themselves into a meditative state. In *Kung Fu: History, Philosophy and Technique,* authors David Chow and Richard Spangler assert that t'ai chi ch'uan may be considered to be the ultimate "moving meditation." Created by Taoist priest Chang San-fen, this martial art has gained widespread popularity throughout the world, and especially in its native China, where thousands of people (some in their nineties) can be seen practicing in parks every morning. T'ai chi ch'uan develops the leg muscles, as well as balancing and centering skills. The slowness of the movements forces students to execute them precisely and correctly, and thus helps improve concentration and focus. This is somewhat like playing a piano piece slowly, so that finger movements must be carefully controlled and any mistakes will be obvious; it is much easier to race through a piece, so that imperfections are less easily noticed.

As we have seen above, Ed Parker endorsed the value of katas, believing in a structured approach to his kenpo system; Bruce Lee, the creator of jeet kune do, emphasized the freedom of his system, and claimed not to use katas. Even though they approached their respective arts from different perspectives, these men were both great pioneers in the martial arts and highly proficient in the systems they developed. There have even been successful martial artists who never practiced katas, some even ridiculing them or claiming they have no practical value. Bill ("Superfoot") Wallace, a former world kickboxing champion, believes that katas are beautiful to watch, but would probably never be used in a real-life situation. He also claims that they do nothing for timing and distancing, two skills that he believes can only be worked on with a partner.

While it is true that actual forms would not be used during an attack, they are a means to becoming proficient on the street. Both forms and sets focus on specific movements—kicking, blocking, striking—and thus contain the martial artist's "menus" of motion. As in a restaurant, we don't order the entire menu, but select what suits us at the moment. The English alphabet provides another analogy. When writing, we never use its twenty-six letters in the original order we learned them; we rather select and combine them to create limitless variations for successfully communicating. Likewise, in a self-defense situation we would select from the katas the moves that would be the most effective.

Practicing forms enhances self-defense techniques because all such techniques require various combinations of foot maneuvers, blocking, and striking, which are in turn all elements of the katas. When during a private lesson one student did not remember the upward block called for in one of the self-defense techniques, the instructor reminded him by calling out "Blocking set one!" The student smiled and reflexively performed the upward block called for in the set, then quickly incorporated it into the self-defense technique.

With regard to improving timing and distancing, there are specific foot maneuvers in katas that are utilized to modify the distance between attacker and defender. The kenpo system, for example, incorporates movements called push-drags, step-throughs, crossovers, and pull-drags for such purposes. There are also elements of katas that are practiced to improve timing, which is so critical in self-defense techniques.

Howard Frydman, a third-degree black belt in shotokan and a teacher of martial arts to children, believes that kata practice does indeed develop self-defense skills. However, he does not worry that proficiency in forms will make children prone to fighting. "The ones that are going to misuse martial arts don't have the proper respect, and could never take the discipline [to master the forms]. All they want to do is fight. Thank God they never develop their basics and katas, because this is the only way you can develop tremendous technique. Katas develop the reflexes needed for fighting. You may develop reflexes if you just fight, but you'll never develop speed and power; you'll never develop devastating kicks unless you emphasize heavy basic work, which incorporates stances, kicking, punching, and repetitions. Someone may know how to fight by fighting a little bit (and know about punching and kicking), but if he just wants to fight, he won't be doing the necessary repetitions."

Moreover, as mentioned earlier, as students picture their opponents during kata practice, their visualization skills are constantly being developed. In some katas, students must imagine they are being attacked from different directions by multiple opponents. This could be useful against real threats, which can come from more than one direction. Aside from practical applications, however, the diligent practice of forms develops balance, stamina, speed, and power. It is possible to become a good athlete or martial artist without forms, but with forms, one will become that much better.

For parents unfamiliar with the training and activities of specific martial arts, observing kata practice is a good way to get a feel for the basic nature of an art. Because forms incorporate the strikes, kicks, blocks, punches, parries, foot maneuvers, and even actual self-defense techniques, each serves as a microcosm of the art. Watching forms practice will then teach parents what their children will be learning should they choose to study that particular martial art. Of course, no two children will move exactly alike; each child will exhibit his or her own special individuality. However, with practice, they will come to display the true qualities inculcated by all kata: beauty, power, and grace.

# UNDERSTANDING STYLES AND SYSTEMS

*The training, in and of itself, is a path to the philosophy. Simply by training, by being on time, by bowing and showing respect, the tenets of the martial arts in time naturally become part of one's life, because of the discipline needed to train every day and the necessity to adhere to the moral code.*

—Hee Il Cho
tae kwon do master
1989 Instructor of the Year, *Black Belt* Hall of Fame

Once a child has expressed an interest in studying a martial art, and his or her parents have been convinced of the merits of such an activity (hopefully with the assistance of this book), they will next be faced with the seemingly daunting task of choosing a martial art, a school, and an instructor. This and the following chapter will provide parents with what they need to know to make the wisest possible choices.

## Styles and Systems

When we discuss a martial art style, we are referring to the country, region, or nationality of its origin. Some well-known styles include: Chinese, Okinawan, Japanese, Korean, Southeast Asian, Brazilian, and American. In most of these styles, many systems (or disciplines within the style) have been developed. Systems are sometimes named after their founders or the villages or regions where they were developed; others have descriptive names thought to summarize the essential characteristics of the systems.

Styles and systems are sometimes also categorized into four main types: grappling arts, striking arts, kicking arts, and spiritual arts. For example: judo is considered a grappling art; karate a striking art; tae kwon do a kicking art; and t'ai chi ch'uan a spiritual art. As there are probably as many martial arts systems than there are spoken languages, the list of styles and systems presented here is not meant to be exhaustive, but includes some well-known martial arts and those for which instruction is available in the West.

## Chinese Systems

Although often thought of as a system, kung fu (meaning "skill" or "ability") is actually the generic name that Westerners use to refer to the Chinese martial arts. Kung fu's many styles place a great emphasis on the imitation of the movements, spirit, and fighting tactics of birds, snakes, insects, and land animals; the essence of particular animals has subsequently been incorporated into the disciplines and fighting techniques, in order to maximize both health and fighting ability. *Wu shu* (meaning "martial art") is the official term for martial arts used in the People's Republic of China. Although used interchangeably with kung fu, *wu shu* is also the name of a particular system, known for its dynamic acrobatic movements. To avoid confusion, one must be aware of the context in which the term is being used.

Chinese martial arts are often classified as Northern or Southern styles. Within these styles, individual systems are often referred to as external ("hard") or internal ("soft") arts. External systems focus on physical strength, while internal systems focus on the cultivation of *ch'i*. Bodhidharma is believed to be the father of kung fu. This Indian prince, who became a monk, wandered into China during the sixth century A.D., and settled at the Shaolin Monastery, where he taught meditation as a way to enlightenment. Feeling that meditation alone did not address the needs of the body for physical fitness and development, he designed eighteen hand movements to be practiced while standing in place. These movements evolved into what became known as Shaolin Temple Boxing, an embryonic stage of kung fu.

Shaolin Temple Boxing spread throughout China, and materialized in a variety of forms, with a clear North-South division. Northern Shaolin specializes in long-range fighting, emphasizing kicking techniques over hand techniques. Being generally taller than their Southern counterparts, the Northerners take advantage of their longer legs. They exhibit constant movement in an array of spinning, jumping, and sweeping movements. Southern Shaolin is based on the original Shaolin Temple boxing, emphasizing hand techniques, with deep horse stances and many stretching exercises utilized in training. *Chi-na* ("seize and control") techniques are also employed.

Shaolin five animal kung fu, an external and internal system, is based on the movements and distinctive features of the dragon, tiger, leopard, snake, and crane, with forms and self-defense techniques imitating their movements and characteristics. The external training is based on the tiger and the leopard, both known for strength, power, speed, and balance. Internal training is based on the crane, snake, and dragon, known for patience, *ch'i* energy, and soft circular movements.

There are many different styles of t'ai chi ch'uan ("grand ultimate fist"), which is practiced in China as well as all over the world. Known as an internal system, the slow, fluid, and circular movements improve circulation, muscle control, breathing, and overall health. That it promotes longevity, as the Chinese believe, can be supported by the many people well into their nineties who practice this art religiously. Although many people do not regard t'ai chi ch'uan as a martial art, its movements can be utilized as a highly effective means of self-defense. Two exercises called *tui sao* ("pushing hands") and *chan si kung* ("silk-reeling skill") are exercises that, in conjunction with the forms, help unlock the internal power of the art, and enhance the self-defense applications.

*Pa kua* (also spelled and pronounced *ba gua*) means "eight trigrams" and is an internal system based on the the theory of the *I Ching (Book of Changes)*. This Chinese boxing system utilizes circular paths of travel in its hand techniques and foot maneuvers. Many of its techniques are effective at close or long range. Palm strikes are the primary weapon, and kicks are seldom used. Training focuses on firm and rapid walking, which in conjunction with its elusive movements, tends to baffle opponents. In conformity with its spiritual elements, the pa-kua stylist considers the development of *ch'i* to be its highest goal.

*Wing chun* ("glorious springtime"), an external system founded by a woman named Mg Mui, is the system that Bruce Lee first studied, under Yip Man. In this economical and efficient system, each offensive maneuver can simultaneously serve as a defensive maneuver, and vice versa. *Wing chun* stylists advance on their opponents with forward energy and momentum, smothering them with rapid hand techniques. By following the centerline of their body and delivering all strikes based on the principle that the shortest distance between two points is a straight line, the *wing chun* stylist can not only strike faster, but deflect his opponent's non centerline attacks. "Trapping" is developed through training in *chi sao* ("sticky hands"). When contact is made, the *wing chun* stylist "sticks" to his opponent's strikes while jamming and trapping his limbs. Weapons training and forms practice round out this well-balanced system.

*Choy li fut* is an external system which utilizes long-range fighting techniques. In this system, power originates from the waist through strong, low horse stances. This southern style is best known for its powerful whipping and slashing movements, as well as for its use of uppercuts, backhand fists, knuckle punches, hammerfists, and roundhouse strikes. Because its techniques are practiced with maximum extension, it is also a good system for developing flexibility and physical fitness.

## Okinawan Systems

The origins of many of our present-day karate systems can be traced back to sixteenth-century Okinawa, the largest of the Ryukyu Islands. Lying between Japan and China, Okinawa was a major center of trade, and because of the continuous economic contact between the Okinawan and Chinese people, many religious and cultural ideas came to be shared. Many Okinawan karate masters traveled to China to study kung fu and, as a result, the Okinawans developed their own martial art, referred to as *te* (hand). *Shuri-te, naha-te,* and *tomari-te* were three original systems, and eventually, *kara-te* ("China hand") became the term used to refer to the many systems that evolved from these.

*Shorin-ryu* is one of the Okinawan karate systems still practiced today that directly evolved from *shuri-te* and *tomari-te.* This system utilizes both hard and soft techniques, with a focus on the hands for blocking and striking. Kicking is generally done below the waist, and the practice of kata is stressed.

*Goju-ryu* ("hard-soft way") was developed by Chojun Miyagi, an Okinawan who took his system (a combination of hard Okinawan karate and soft Chinese forms) to Japan. This system was depicted in the extremely popular 1984 movie *The Karate Kid*, in which Mr. Miyagi, the character played be Noriyuki "Pat" Morita, has the same last name as the actual founder of the system. *Goju-ryu* is known for its deep abdominal breathing, which is utilized in its katas. The system aims to synchronize the hand and foot maneuvers in conjunction with the breathing, and is characterized by upright stances, short foot maneuvers, and close-range fighting techniques.

*Uechi-ryu* was founded and named by Kanbum Uechi, an Okinawan who studied kung fu in China for thirteen years. In 1910, he returned to Okinawa, and developed the "hard-soft" system that takes his name. It is often referred to as the "sister" system of *goju-ryu*. Both systems utilize the *sanchin* kata, designed to harden the entire body through deep abdominal breathing. Although there are slight differences, this kata is performed in a similar manner in both systems. It is practiced without the *gi* (uniform) top, allowing the instructor to visually check proper body tension. When performed correctly, the practitioner is able to withstand powerful blows to the body without sustaining injuries. This system is characterized by the use of fingertip strikes, one-knuckle punches, kicking with the big toe rather than the ball of the foot, and circular blocks.

Okinawan karate master Choki Motubu is considered to be the father of *shorei-ryu,* whose origins can be traced back to the Shaolin Temple. *Shorei-ryu,* as well as many of the Okinawan systems, profited from close ties with nearby China. The evidence of this strong influence can be seen in *Shorei-ryu's* use of the animals used in the Shaolin five animal kung-fu system. This system emphasizes six martial arts weapons: the *bo* (a five to six foot staff made of hard wood); *sai* (a short forklike metal weapon with three prongs of unequal length); *nunchaku* (two hardwood sticks of equal length connected by a rope or chain); *tonfa* (a fifteen to twenty inch piece of hard wood gripped by a short, protruding handle); *kama* (a short blade, similar to a sickle, which is set perpendicular to a hardwood handle approximately eighteen inches in length); and *teko* (similar to brass knuckles).

*Issin-ryu* was founded by Tatsuo Shimabuko, who incorporated what he felt were the best features of *shorin-ryu* and *goju-ryu.* This system stresses economy of motion, kicking below the waist, an equal emphasis on the hands and feet, the utilization of defensive maneuvers as offensive weapons, and vice versa. One of the primary weapons is the vertical punch, which, as are other techniques, is snapped back without reaching full extension.

## Japanese Systems

The martial arts in Japan have been around for hundreds of years. Jujutsu (also spelled jiu jitsu and jujitsu) was the term often used for the various systems that developed from the Japanese samurai. It is believed that the Japanese grappling arts had their origins in sumo. Jujutsu was first developed in seventeenth century Japan, and means "the technique of suppleness." Jujutsu emphasizes throws, checks, and joint-locks, and also utilizes kicking, striking, and grappling. It is the "mother" system of judo and Brazilian jujutsu. There are many forms of jujutsu, with *daito-ryu aiki-jutsu* (which supplemented empty-hand techniques with weapons) being one of the earliest. This was the form of jujutsu studied by Morihei Ueshiba, the founder of aikido.

Karate was introduced to Japan in 1922 during a demonstration by Gichin Funakoshi, the founder of the shotokan system and father of Japanese karate. He originally introduced karate to the Japanese physical education program, and assigned Japanese names to replace the Okinawan names of the katas. Feeling that the Japanese people should have their own indigenous martial art, he decided to change the meaning of the Okinawan term, "kara-te" ("China hand") to the Japanese translation of karate ("empty hand").

Judo ("gentle way") was the first martial art to be included as an Olympic sport in 1964. Founded in 1882 by Jigoro Kano, a student of jujutsu, this system specializes in throwing and grappling techniques. Although it can be used as a highly effective system of self-defense, it is primarily practiced as a sport. Like jujutsu, it utilizes chokes and joint-locking techniques, but employs much more grappling. Although a full-contact sport, safety and respect for others is always stressed. The two main principles emphasized are "maximum efficiency" and "mutual benefit and welfare."

Aikido ("the way of harmony with the spirit") was founded in 1942 by Morihei Ueshiba, who incorporated the teachings of *daito-ryu aiki-jutsu* and *kenjutsu* ("art of the sword") as the root of his system. O-Sensei, as Ueshiba was respectfully called, developed aikido in conformity with his religious ideals. This system places great emphasis on the unification of the mind and body while employing the concept of *ki* (the Japanese pronunciation of the Chinese *ch'i*). There are no formal blocking techniques; instead, an opponent's force and energy are used against him. He is subdued by an array of wrist and joint-locks, and dynamic throwing techniques. The training drills include: footwork, parrying, rolling, and falling, all practiced with many repetitions, in order to achieve perfection. Since Ueshiba first developed aikido, many derivative systems have come into existence. Never intended to be a sport, this peaceful art was developed only as a means of self-defense.

Shotokan ("hall of Shoto") derives its name from the pen name of its founder, Gichin Funakoshi. This system places a strong emphasis on dynamic body movements and on the principle that rotation, shifting, forward momentum, and the contraction and relaxation of the muscles increase power. Training is initially done in deep stances in order to develop balance as well as strength in the legs and hips. As one becomes more proficient, the stances become higher so as to increase mobility. Powerful hip rotation is utilized in its punching, blocking, and kicking techniques, and fighting drills and kata play an integral role in one's training.

Japanese *goju-ryu* ("hard-soft way") developed when Okinawan *goju-ryu* master Chojun Miyagi brought his system to Japan at the invitation of Gogen "the Cat" Yamaguchi, to teach at Ritsumeikan University. Before Miyagi returned to Okinawa, he awarded Yamaguchi, who became the head instructor of the karate club at the university, the highest rank in *goju-ryu.* Yamaguchi went on to develop his own system, known as Japanese *goju-ryu*, based on the Okinawan system he had learned. It is characterized by its strikes and kicks, which are delivered in rapid succession. So as to be able to strike an opponent from any angle, much side to side weaving movement is employed. *Goju-ryu* is known for its circular movements and deep abdominal breathing. Kata and sparring are integral parts of the system.

*Shito-ryu* was founded by Kenwa Mabuni in the 1930s. He had studied karate with some of Okinawa's greatest masters, in addition to kung fu from a Chinese merchant living in Okinawa. This system places equal emphasis on the study of basics, sparring, and kata, of which there are over forty. Similar to shotokan, *shito-ryu* stylists utilize the reverse punch and front kick as their primary weapons, but train in a more upright stance. In conformity with its Okinawan roots, *kobu-jutsu* ("weapons arts") are also an integral part of the system.

*Kyokushinkai* was named in 1961 by its founder, Masutatsu ("Mas") Oyama. Born Hyung Ye in Korea in 1923, Oyama was sent at age fourteen to attend a military academy in Japan, where he adopted his Japanese name. Soon after his arrival he began studying *shotokan,* and several years later, *goju-ryu.* Through intensive training he became proficient in both karate systems, and decided to combine what he believed were the most effective elements of each into a new system, *kyokushinkai.* Known as a "hard" fighting system, students are taught that heavy body contact, without the use of protective equipment, will help them overcome the fear of getting hit. This system places an equal emphasis on basics, kata, sparring, and *tameshiwari* (breaking skills). Oyama felt that breaking solid objects, such as tiles and bricks, was an excellent means by which to focus one's fighting spirit and develop *ki.*

## Korean Systems

Because of its close proximity to China and Japan, Korea was greatly influenced by the martial arts that were practiced in these two countries. During the Silla period (mid-seventh to mid-tenth centuries), the *hwarang* warriors trained in a form of hand-to-hand combat called *hwarang-do.* Won Gwang, a Buddhist monk, is said to have developed this first Korean martial art. *Tae kyon* was developed during the later Yi dynasty, ultimately becoming the art known today as *tae kwon do,* so named by General Choi-Hong-hi.

Yong Shul Choi is said to have studied *daito-ryu aiki-jutsu* in Japan in the early twentieth century. When he came back to his native Korea, he combined this

Japanese system with that of *hwarang-do* and *tae-kyon* to form *hapkido*.

In the late 1940s, Hwang Kee founded his own system. This grandmaster, who had studied kung fu in China, combined elements of the Chinese martial arts with that of *tae kyon* and *soo bahk do* to form *tang soo do moo duk kwan*. (In the names of many Korean martial arts, the term *kwan*, meaning "school," is used.)

*Hwarang-do* ("way of flowering youth") practitioners follow a set of precepts: loyalty, trust, courage, and justice. This "hard-soft" system utilizes thousands of offensive and defensive techniques. Linear and circular movements are emphasized in the strikes, blocks, and kicks. Joint manipulation and pressure point techniques are stressed, as well as an understanding of the human anatomy. The study of weapons are incorporated in the system, and the ability to control inner energy *(ki,* the Korean term for *ch'i)* is practiced through the use of meditation and breathing exercises.

Tae kwon do ("art of kicking and punching") was named as the national sport of Korea in 1945, and in 1988 was introduced as a demonstration sport at the Olympic games in Seoul. This system utilizes strikes, blocks, jumps, and spinning techniques, with a great emphasis placed on flexibility and dynamic linear and circular kicking combinations. Both forms and a variety of self-defense techniques can be found in this highly popular system, which is sometimes referred to as *tae kwon do moo duk kwan*.

*Hapkido* ("way of coordinated power") combines elements of Japanese and Korean martial arts. It is based on three principles: circular movements, the countering of attacks, and the borrowing of an opponent's force. Joint-locks, throws, strikes, kicks, and pressure-point techniques are prevalent throughout the system. The practice of forms and the development of *ki* also play an important role.

*Tang soo do* ("way of the China hand") combined the "hard" elements of traditional Korean martial arts with the "soft" elements of Northern Chinese Style to create this "hard-soft" system. A greater emphasis is placed on the use of kicks than on hands, but an equal emphasis is placed on the practice of forms and self-defense techniques. This system, also known as *tang soo do soo bahk do moo duk kwan,* stresses the "spiritual" as opposed to the "sport" aspects, and the development of character through the integration of the mind, body, and spirit.

## Southeast Asian Styles

Martial arts have been practiced in Southeast Asia for centuries. Many of their roots can be traced back to the cultural and martial art influences of China and India. Within Southeast Asian styles are hundreds of systems, usually named after the villages where they originated, or after their founders. The spiritual qualities of many of these arts stem from the influences of Buddhism and Islam. Music, as an accompaniment to the training and practice of forms and drills, also plays an important role in most Southeast Asian styles.

*Kali* (also known as *arnis* and *escrima)* is the "mother art" of Filipino martial arts. Developed in the Philippines, this system is best known for its bladed weapons and wooden or rattan sticks. Empty hands can also be utilized while executing palm, finger, and elbow strikes, in addition to knuckle punches, traps, and locks. Footwork, of great importance in this system, utilizes various patterns of movement, which follow the geometric lines of the triangle. While kicking, an emphasis is placed on striking the lower portion of the legs. Some of the training methods are: "flow drills" to increase one's fluidity, the practice of *sinawali* (the weaving patterns of two sticks), and freestyle sparring. Although there is a sporting aspect to this system, this art is a serious form of self-defense.

*Pencak* (also spelled *pentjak*) *Silat* is the indigenous art of Indonesia. In Malaysia, it is usually called *silat*. There are hundreds of different types of systems within the Malay archipelago. Considered arts of self-preservation, these combat-oriented systems are too dangerous to be practiced as a sport. Although defensive in nature, they follow the philosophy that one should attack the attacker; practitioners utilize their entire bodies, borrowing their attacker's motion and energy without retreating. Their many techniques include punches, kicks, elbows, knees, trapping, joint-locking, and grappling. A variety of weapons (particularly bladed weapons) are used throughout these systems.

*Muay Thai* (also called Thai kickboxing) was developed and has been practiced in Thailand for centuries. The country's most treasured sport, one which does not utilize forms, is also an effective system of self-defense. Training is very intense, with a great emphasis placed on the utilization of the entire body to "follow through" with kicks, the most devastating of which is the roundhouse kick. Opponents can expect to receive a barrage of punches, elbows, and knees, coming from all angles.

## Brazilian Systems

Brazilian martial arts date back hundreds of years, from the time slaves from Africa were brought to Brazil. When they first arrived, they developed a fighting system that formed the roots of what was to become *capoeira*. Originally intended as a self-defense system, the practice of this art was prohibited by the slave owners. To disguise the combat element, the slaves incorporated the movements into their indigenous music, dance, and songs. Ninety percent of the *capoeira* system's techniques consist of kicking or leg sweeping movements. Acrobatic movements such as handstands and cartwheels are used to deliver strikes to the head. Forms are not utilized. The movements performed during practice are not choreographed, and are usually done in the *hoda* (circle) to musical accompaniment. The system is graceful and dance-like, with an emphasis placed on the sporting and exercise elements. It is nonetheless a highly effective self-defense system, which is enhanced by its deceptive movements.

A Brazilian martial art influenced by a Japanese system was devised in the early twentieth century. The Gracie family had helped Japanese immigrants establish a Japanese community in Brazil. In doing so, Gastao Gracie met a Japanese jujutsu champion named Mitsuo Maeda Koma. Grateful for what the Gracies had done for him, Koma agreed to teach jujutsu to Carlos Gracie, the son of Gastao. Because this art was only meant to be taught to the Japanese, Carlos had to agree that its secrets would be kept within the Gracie family. After Koma's death, however, Carlos felt that his obligation to his sensei had been fulfilled, and began teaching this art to the general public; it evolved into the system known today as Gracie jujutsu.

Gracie jujutsu is a hybrid system focusing on ground fighting techniques. It utilizes the striking, grappling, throwing and joint-locking techniques from its Japanese roots, and has also borrowed from boxing, karate, and other systems. According to the Gracies, if a technique improves their system, they will incorporate it. This pure self-defense system utilizes over seven hundred techniques, and is based on the belief that most fights go to the ground.

## American Systems

Karate was introduced to the United States in the mid 1940s, but it was not until the early 1950s that Ed Parker, a Hawaiian who had studied kenpo with Professor William K.S. Chow, began to teach this "Americanized" system on the mainland United States. Feeling that the traditional karate systems would not be effective on the streets of modern-day America, Parker (now known as the "father of American kenpo karate") revised and experimented with the kenpo he had learned, to create practical concepts and principles of self-defense.

American kenpo karate is known for the blinding speed of its multiple hand strikes and explosive self-defense techniques. Specific sets are practiced to enhance specific skills, such as stances, blocking, kicking, and striking. Forms and sparring also play an integral role in this system. An equal emphasis is placed on the utilization of the hands and feet. Linear, angular, and circular movements combine in infinite combinations to create a perpetual state of motion.

In 1967, Bruce Lee named the system he developed jeet kune do ("way of the intercepting fist"). Lee, who had studied *wing chun* in China, came to the United States in the early 1960s, and began to dissect numerous other systems in order to incorporate the most practical elements of their training methods and combat theories into his own system. His incessant thirst for knowledge led him to create a new and constantly evolving American system.

Jeet kune do integrates the Filipino, Indonesian, Thai, Chinese, and Western martial arts. Although JKD utilizes training methods and combat theories from all these arts, it incorporates no forms. Bruce Lee viewed combat efficiency as the most important goal of the martial artist. Practitioners of this system modify their techniques to conform to the infinite number of fighting scenarios which may arise. JKD's principle of range encompasses these scenarios. The four stages are: kicking range, punching range, trapping range, and grappling range.

Chuck Norris, one of the great American champions, won almost every major karate championship between 1965 and 1970. Aside from his competitive spirit, Norris was and is a perpetual student of the martial arts. He constantly seeks out the masters of other systems, then uses what they teach him to improve his fighting skills. Since 1982, when he formed the U.F.A.F. (United Fighting Arts Federation), members of his federation referred to his fighting style as the Chuck Norris system. Like jeet kune do, Norris's system, given the name *chun kuk do* (the "universal way") in the early 1990s, is constantly evolving.

*Chun kuk do* reflects its Korean roots. Chuck Norris, who had studied *tang soo do,* utilizes the kicking elements of this system. In addition, he incorporates the hand techniques of the traditional Japanese karate systems and the grappling techniques of Brazilian jujutsu. The influences of kickboxing and judo are also present. Traditional philosophies as well as forms are also incorporated into this well-balanced system.

True martial artists are always asking: "What can I do to improve my art?" In the process of refining their skills, they have frequently modified their systems by incorporating techniques of other systems, or combined what they believed were the most effective maneuvers of several systems, resulting in many derivatives of the original systems. Although the criticism "watered down" has been leveled at some of these newer arts, in fact this evolution has been going on throughout the history of martial arts. As Bruce Lee said: "A style should never be considered gospel truth, the laws and principles of which can never be violated. Man, the living, creating individual, is always more important than any style."

## Systems and Body Types

Because there are so many systems, the child and parent are faced with an abundance of alternatives. Some martial artists believe that a system should be geared to a body type; they would suggest that tae kwon do is ideal for very limber children, because of its emphasis on flexibility and high kicking. Short, stocky children would do well with judo, because a low center of gravity is an advantage. Aikido, a system which emphasizes leverage and using an opponent's strength against him, might be suitable for smaller, slighter children.

We asked shotokan instructor Howard Frydman, a third-degree black belt, if certain styles or systems are better for certain body types. "I believe that is correct," he said. "Shotokan and other Japanese systems seem to be suited for all body types, but if you had to pick, these might be best for really strong people who are shorter and lower to the ground. But any person can learn shotokan. In tae kwon do, on the other hand, a lanky and flexible body type, preferably with small hips, is better suited, because a lot of kicking, including jump kicking, is required."

For this reason, Mr. Frydman would not recommend tae kwon do for overweight and unlimber children, even if they were highly motivated. "I think that when doing jump kicks, the chance of hurting their knees or ankles would be greatly increased. In addition, most people who are overweight have back problems, so it's just a question of when problems will develop. Jumping up and crashing down with all that weight hurts the ankles, back, and knees. An overweight kid who is motivated, and has a good teacher, however, could still do great in a Japanese system. Shotokan training, for example, can be started at any age; if you're not flexible, that's OK, because a front kick is all you really have to master. A side kick, which requires more flexibility, can be mastered to the knee. In general, Japanese systems develop the hands and feet evenly."

In response to the question of whether a system such as tae kwon do might not be appropriate for an extremely overweight and unlimber kid, Dr. Abrams replied: "I would never say that. I think that's more a function of the teacher, because even if the kid is obese, if he's training, he's going to develop flexibility and coordination, and he's going to lose weight. I've seen obese people and incredibly muscle-bound people with flexibility that I wish I had. It isn't so much the body type, size, or anything else that matters; I think the most important thing is what you feel most comfortable with."

There are no right or wrong answers to these questions. Two highly proficient martial artists may have different views on an issue, but both views may be equally valid depending upon the circumstances. Moreover, every child is different. Some may do certain things with more natural ease than other children, and vice versa. A motivated child who is not talented in a given activity can become talented through hard work. At five feet four inches tall, Muggsy Bogues was supposed to be too short to play professional basketball, but has been playing in the NBA since 1987. His speed, ball handling ability and savvy has enabled him to succeed in the land of the giants.

We believe that even children with the "wrong" body type can probably do very well in any system that they have a great interest in. Hard work can make up for practically any physical shortcoming, and progress will certainly be greater than that of children with the "right" body type who lack interest and do not practice. We would draw the line, however, at recommending tae kwon do for a very overweight and unlimber child. This is not to say that with much discipline and hard work, a child could not improve his or her flexibility and lose weight in the process, but we fear the initial frustration might be too difficult to overcome. Indeed, frustration could easily lead a child to reject all martial arts or even all physical activity. We believe that children should get involved in what they can most readily become engaged in and make progress in.

Sometimes a children's hospital or rehabilitation center will recommend martial arts for children with disabilities, severe handicaps, or coordination problems. Kung fu, which requires a lot of acrobatics and fairly good coordination, might not be a good choice for this purpose; a basic karate style that teaches blocks and strikes in a general way would be more appropriate.

## Systems and Personalities

Are there systems more compatible with a particular emotional makeup or personality? Again, there are no hard and fast answers, but for a child who has shown aggressive tendencies, aikido might be a better choice than an attack-oriented system such as kickboxing. The latter might reinforce aggressive tendencies, whereas aikido teaches movements that employ the energy of an attack to deflect the danger harmlessly away. Morihei Ueshiba, the founder of the system, once stated, "The purpose of aikido is to bring peace to the world."

Another less aggressive art is t'ai chi ch'uan. Although the movements of this graceful art are based on fighting techniques, its martial aspects are often deemphasized. On the other hand, its movements do not make the strong physical demands of systems such as tae kwon do and *goju-ryu,* so those looking for a real workout for physical conditioning may be disappointed. Although most kids like to roughhouse, some may be uncomfortable with either delivering or receiving punches. For these children, a grappling art such as judo, rather than tae kwon do or *goju-ryu,* may be more appropriate.

As mentioned in the previous chapter, the best way to gauge the demands the art might place on a child physically and mentally is to watch a practice session. Taking the child along with you should allow you to judge, from comments and reactions, how suitable the art is for him or her.

# CHOOSING AN INSTRUCTOR AND SCHOOL

*In your business dealings you express your values and objectives. It is not only important to make money . . . You must have principles. Any truly successful businessman understands martial arts ideals and martial artists understand those of business. The objectives may be different but human values are the same."*

—Teruyuki Okazaki
chairman and chief instructor
International Shotokan Karate Federation
1982 Man of the Year, *Black Belt* Hall of Fame

Once a martial art is decided upon, parents are faced with the task of finding an appropriate instructor and school. The first question you will want answered, but perhaps the most difficult to answer, is "Is the instructor qualified?" When we go to a doctor, we want and expect a high level of expertise, which can be verified by credentials. This is not always the case in the world of martial arts. Anyone with the means can open a school, and call it Joe's Fighting Academy, and often these schools are better as businesses than as places of serious martial arts study. It is not unusual for a teacher to have a self-designated ranking. On the other hand, just because an instructor is teaching in his basement does not mean that he or she is not qualified; for many years, Bruce Lee did not own a school.

As when choosing a doctor, the best method, or at least a method that will give you peace of mind, is to get a recommendation from other parents, and perhaps talk to their children who are students. This is usually easy, since many children choose to study a martial art because a friend is doing it; find out who the friend is and speak to his or her parents. When you get a recommendation, call the school and speak directly with the person who will be teaching your child. Although it might be more difficult to check a martial art instructor's credentials than a doctor's, answers to the following questions should give you some idea and should be asked:

What rank or belt level does the instructor hold?
What organization or school awarded the ranking?
How many years has the instructor studied the art?
With whom did the instructor study?
How long has the instructor been teaching?
Where has the instructor previously taught?
What awards has the instructor won?
What is the instructor's competition experience?
How long has the school been open?
Is the instructor open, frank, and friendly?
Will the instructor gladly let you observe a class?
Will the instructor be available to answer questions?

Next, visit the school. "Go in and visit the instructor," says Tom Festa, a fifth-degree black belt and teacher of tae kwon do, "see what his goals are for the children. Check his credentials, and see that the system he's teaching is accredited. You may want to call some people who are studying that system, simply because there's no regulating body that stops people from opening schools, and we have to safeguard our children."

"Visit the school," Mr. Festa continues, "think of how much time you're going to spend when you select a college for your child. You're going to visit schools, check them out and see that they have the right curriculum for your child's interests. Do the same with martial arts schools, because we actually shape your children's minds and help *prepare* them for college."

A head instructor and owner of a school should have some type of diploma and hold at least a third-degree black belt; preferably, he or she will still be under the tutelage of a senior instructor. "When you've got your first-degree black belt," says Mr. Festa, "you've mastered some techniques. You've gone out there and experimented, and you've competed. You've *tasted* martial arts. You then showed that determination to move on; you got a second degree. It's kind of like getting your bachelor's degree, and then deciding that you want a master's degree, and then a doctorate. At this point, a third-degree black belt will be thinking about teaching other people."

Although rank and expertise in one's art are important, Mr. Festa points out that these are not absolute criteria. "I'm not really concerned with rank that much," he says. "To be classed as a 'legitimate' instructor I suppose a third-degree black belt counts for something. But there are probably some first-degree black belts who are more capable as teachers than some tenth-degree black belts, who may be very, very good at the art itself but who don't have the ability to teach as well."

In addition to querying the instructor directly, some outside sources may be able to give you some information. The Better Business Bureau and the local Chamber of Commerce should be able to tell you whether there have been any complaints regarding business practices. Most reputable instructors and schools are affiliated with established organizations. Some examples are: the International Chinese Kuoshu Federation (I.C.K.F.); the International Kenpo Karate Association (I.K.K.A.); the Japanese Karate Association (J.K.A.); and the Amateur Athletic Union (A.A.U.). In addition to these organizations are the Martial Arts for Peace Association (M.A. P.A.), a program aimed at resolving conflicts through peaceful means; and the Kick Drugs Out of America Foundation (K.D.O.O.A.). This non-profit organization uses martial arts philosophy to teach children moral values, and educates them to resist peer pressure to experiment with drugs or join street gangs. Founded by actor and martial arts master Chuck Norris, its programs have been integrated into the Texas public school system.

Even if you have a recommendation for a particular school, visit several; comparing them will allow you to make a more informed decision. Even if you know nothing about the martial arts, you will likely come away with a fairly correct impression of what you observed. Gut instincts are often a very reliable measuring stick. Specific points to observe on your visit are:

What is the condition of the school?
Is it kept neat and clean?
Is it properly lit and well-ventilated?
Is it bright and cheerful, or depressing?
Do student-instructor relationships seem congenial?
Do the students display any forms of dojo etiquette?
Are rules regarding respect for the dojo observed?
Do students seem to be alert and involved?
Is practice conducted with energy and dedication?
Is the activity level suitable for your child?
How big are the classes?
What is the level of supervision?
Are students getting enough individual attention?

The following questions are more difficult to ascertain directly, but you will likely get some feel for them:

Is the spiritual component of the art presented?
Is respect for good values evident or referred to?
Is loyalty to the school, instructor, and system evident?

What should an instructor be like when a parent walks into a school? "First of all," says Tom Festa, "he should be friendly. And he should be accessible. The idea of some instructors that they are above speaking to parents, that parents should speak to some 'assistant' or 'program manager,' is to me simply absurd. I believe that the head instructor should meet the parents, know all about the students in the school, and about their growth and progress . . . Parents have sometimes told me of visiting schools where they can't speak to the head instructor, who will usually have some great name like 'grandmaster' or 'grand pupon'. When I hear these stories I shake my head and wonder why anyone would spend their dollars to support such places."

The instructor should ideally be approachable for personal problems and concerns outside the dojo. After all, martial arts are inseparable from life, and as with other sports, an instructor is often seen as a mentor or even a father figure by young students. His or her character, both inside and outside the dojo, is important.

"The instructor's background," says judo instructor Jack Krystek, "is important, and not just in the art. What he does in his *life* is also important. You might have a champion whose head is not quite there teaching your kids. Not everyone is a teacher, and not everyone is a champion, either. If you have both, great, but it doesn't always work out that way. Do you need to be a champion to teach kids? I don't think so."

Is it important that a school or instructor has trained champions? "Not at all," says Dr. Krystek. "Your school might exist for a hundred years without producing a champion. But there might be lots of kids that because of your influence don't wind up dead or in jail. And that is what's important. If kids trust you, you can talk to them, and as a teacher you can influence them quite a bit."

The best instructors are keenly alert to the personal problems of their students, since those problems can easily interfere with the total concentration required in the dojo. "I've given students my phone number," says Dr. Krystek, "so they can call me day or night. I tell any kid with a problem to come and talk to me. I have students well into their twenties who still come to see me."

A good instructor's influence can span many years and even generations. "I had a former student," says Dr. Krystek, "come in to see me, who had left me when he was about eighteen or nineteen. He's in his thirties now, and came in with his five kids to sign up again . . . One of the kids was on prozac, and tried to commit suicide. I had a long talk with him, got him off the drug and now he's doing wonderfully. His dad gives me credit for changing this kid's life, and that makes me feel good."

Ask other students and their parents what they think of the school and the instructor. Observe classes taught by the head instructor and by assistants. Students often desire to enroll in a particular school because of the reputation of a particular instructor; if such is the case, you will want to know whether and when that instructor will be teaching your child.

Watch a beginner's class and an advanced class. "If an instructor does not allow you to view a class, right away you can eliminate that school," says Dr. Roger Russell, a fifth-degree black belt in kenpo. Try to observe a child who is approximately the same age and build as your child and who has been studying for a year or so. The level of skill achieved will be similar to that of your child a year from now; you'll be getting a more realistic impression of what your child is going to learn.

"I don't like dictatorships," says Dr. Russell, "I like schools where the instructor teaches kids to think for themselves. I've gone to schools where the kids aren't allowed to say anything except 'Yes, sir.' They're like military schools, and some people think that's great, but I personally like schools where the kids are more involved. They have a little more fun, they're asked questions, and more of their creative nature is brought out. You want to try to get them to work hard but have fun doing it. This is the atmosphere I suggest that parents look for."

For children from four to six years old, it is preferable that the class size not exceed fifteen to twenty, nor should classes last longer than thirty to forty-five minutes. For children from seven to nine years of age, twenty to twenty-five children should be the maximum class size, and classes should not exceed forty-five minutes to an hour.

The fact that, after observing several schools, both parent and child can walk away with an overall positive feeling about a school and its instructors is a more important consideration than what specific system is being taught. Money is always a consideration, but it is wise to pay more for a competent instructor who your child likes and respects, than to choose another simply because he or she charges less. Most schools will have some kind of introductory program; if, after the designated number of lessons the child is unhappy and you wish to reconsider, you should be able to do so before being locked into a contract. Any instructor or school that tries to pressure you into signing a long-term contract, especially on the first visit, should be avoided.

## The Three Most Often Asked Questions

*What is the proper age to begin?* If a child can concentrate, is motivated, is willing to practice, and has supportive parents who will encourage him to practice at home, then we feel that the younger one starts, the better. If a child can speak a language fluently at the age of three, there is no reason why he cannot start martial arts lessons at the age of three or four. If the teacher makes it fun, the child will not consider it burdensome, and will want to learn. Those starting to practice martial arts as middle-aged adults may still develop into highly proficient martial artists if they work hard, but they will never be as good as they would have had they started as children, when the muscles and reflexes are developing, and when the capacity for learning is greatest.

*Should a child be forced to take a martial art?* Most emphatically, no. By all means, expose your child to the martial arts, and encourage him or her to get involved; but if your child doesn't want to do it, don't force him. There are those who will disagree, citing examples of people who were forced to take karate or piano lessons as a child and who, as proficient adults with the benefit of hindsight, have thanked their parents for having the wisdom to firmly direct their childhood actvities. But our view is that the activity itself is less important than the participation, and it is far easier to get children involved in what they like. Parents should keep their eyes open; a child who likes a particular activity will usually show it, and it is better to have a happy ice skater in the family than a miserable martial artist.

*Is it all right to study more than one martial art at a time?* We believe this is not a good idea, since different systems have different principles and techniques, which may even be opposed to each other. One style may teach you to do a kick one way, and another style may teach an apparently similar kick in a different manner. A beginning student, whether a child or adult, could easily get confused.

In their first, basic lessons in martial arts, students are learning to coordinate their bodies; their brains have to learn how to tell their bodies how to move correctly. As Wally Jay, founder of Small Circle Jujutsu, says, "The most important job for students is to find what they are compatible with. But once they start with a system, they should try to stay with it until they master the fundamentals, and not go jumping from one to another. Beginners won't learn much that way; they'll just get confused."

Before branching out, they should probably attain brown or black belt ranking, have a firm grasp of the basics, and have developed a "body memory" through hours and hours of practice. Then if they are taught a new movement in a new system, they will be able to execute it, but also be able to revert at will to the movements they originally learned.

# MARTIAL ARTS AND COMPETITIONS

*For [understanding and promoting] the sport of karate, we have several sources of reference, such as the protective equipment used in other sports, weight classifications, and division into rounds found in boxing, and the types of rules used in Thai boxing. One of the most important factors in spreading karate throughout the world is bringing it before the public eye. Making karate a sport loved by everyone, as well as a martial art, is a fine way to achieve that end.*

—Matsutatsu Oyama,
founder of *kyokushinkai* karate

Should competing in tournaments be mandatory for children studying martial arts? Are tournaments dangerous for younger students? Won't children who fail to win their bouts become discouraged? Isn't the purpose of tournaments simply to develop fighting skills? If parents don't want their children fighting, what is the point of tournament competition?

Many schools heavily promote the competition aspect of the martial arts; other schools shy away from it. We believe competitions are useful, but whether children should compete should be a personal decision— based on their own feelings and goals, as well as the judgment of parents and instructors. Competition is not something that children should be thrust into at the beginning of their training.

Some schools will encourage children to enter tournaments after only six months. Although there are many positive things to be said about competing, we feel this is too soon; such schools tend to base the merit of their art primarily on how well the students do in competition. There is so much more to the martial arts, however; tournaments are just one component of training. Instructors and schools who regard winning at tournaments as the sole purpose of martial arts training can create a false sense of accomplishment in children who succeed and an unwarranted sense of failure in those who do not. As a general rule, we believe children should train for a minimum of a year and acquire some experience in sparring before entering a tournament. This is to ensure that they have a good grasp of the fundamentals. Children who compete without the knowledge of basic foot maneuvers, strikes, and blocks, are more prone to injury.

Tournament pairings are usually random, so it is conceivable that the potential first and second place winners could be matched up against each other in the very first round. "That does happen quite frequently," said Robin Rielly, a sixth-degree black belt in shotokan who often serves as chief referee at such events. "As far as we're concerned," he continued, "this is martial arts, and if you start thinking about it philosophically, there's only first place. In the sword fights in medieval Japan, there was no second place; you either came in first, or were dead. So the fact that the second- and third-best competitors may be eliminated in the early rounds really doesn't make any difference, because ultimately the best would have come in first. Second and third place is nice, and that's sort of a traditional thing with most sports, but if you think about it in terms of martial arts, second and third place really have no meaning."

But couldn't competing and not winning be harmful to a child's confidence and self-esteem? According to Rielly, "As we think of American sports, we think of training to play the game, and training to excel and win the game. In martial arts training, it's just the reverse. The contest itself is really only a kind of training; whether you win or lose is not important, only that you come out and train. We have developed competitions over the years, not because we think they are the end product of our training, but just another part of training. We train in a karate club or dojo day in and day out with people that we're very familiar with. This is a chance to go out under different conditions and test our technique against people we haven't worked out with." To parents who say to him, "I don't know if my child is ready to compete," Rielly responds, "We're not training them to compete; this is only another kind of training. They should just go out and do the best they can."

Contests provide a great learning experience, an environment in which skills can be tested and evaluated. "You enter a contest," Rielly continued, "do very

well, and then 'bang!'—you get hit with a front kick.
What does that tell you? You have a deficiency in your
ability to block a front kick. So now you've identified a
weakness in your technique, or flow. Go back and practice that, and each time you compete, you begin to see
that you need more work in this area or that area." Kids
also get a chance to see other kids at different levels of
proficiency, and a well-disciplined competitor can serve
as an important role model.

In tournaments, competition is usually conducted
in divisions according to skill level: beginner (white,
yellow, and orange belts); intermediate (purple, blue,
and green belts); and advanced (brown, black, and, in
the Korean systems, red belts). There are also gender
and age categories in each division (although younger
boys and girls may sometimes compete against each
other), both in freestyle sparring (kumite) and in kata
(forms), and including those arts using empty hands as
well as weapons. The junior division would include all
those seventeen or younger; very young competitors
(usually four to six years of age), can compete in a pee
wee division. The adult division would include those
eighteen and over. Men compete against men, and
women compete against women; brown belts compete
against brown belts, and black belts compete against
black belts. Participants in kumite compete in various
weight categories: lightweight, middleweight, light
heavyweight, and heavyweight. Since weight is not a
factor in kata competitions, there are no weight classifications.

Tournaments provide children with the exciting
opportunity of competing against each other in both

kata (forms) competition and actual sparring (kumite). Those children who feel uncomfortable about fighting can compete in kata until they become more at ease testing their skills in front of an audience. We believe that both types of competition help children to become more well-rounded and better martial artists.

Sparring can help children get over the fear of being attacked. On a personal note, being a competitor helped co-author Norman Sandler overcome the fear of intimidation. He is small, and was constantly being picked on and bullied while growing up. Performing in front of students and instructors, as well as large groups of people, was very beneficial. He took first place in the very first tournament he competed in. In the next year and a half, however, he competed in fifteen tournaments and lost in every one. Nevertheless, his instructor at the time kept saying, "keep learning, keep training, and you will succeed." As it turned out, he became a successful competitor, so successful in fact, that he became the captain of the United States Karate Team and was on several world championship teams.

Competing did help him, but so did all the other aspects of his karate training. Competitions can be a great adjunct, but they must be put in perspective; it is only one of many types of training, including: self-defense, sets and katas, training in the basics, and fighting drills (which include freestyle sparring). In addition to competing in tournaments, two schools will sometimes compete against each other in a contest known as a *shiai.*

One should enter a competition for the experience, and to have fun. It's not about winning and getting medals; it's about another training session. As long as a good organization is running the tournament, competition can be a wonderful experience. With safety equipment and rules regarding how points are to be scored, children can still practice their fighting skills and improve their reflexes and ability to focus in a relatively safe environment. There is no reason why injuries cannot be kept to a minimum both in the dojo and at a tournament. In addition to safety, sportsmanship and respect—through such acts as bowing to opponents and judges—should be stressed. Competing is an important part of training, but a child who only wants to compete, to the exclusion of all other training activities, is missing the point regarding the true meaning of the martial arts.

"What makes the martial arts so unique," says Tokey Hill, 1980 World Union Karate-do Organization champion and current United States National Team coach, "is that we are one of very few sports that still emphasizes the philosophical background, purity, and respect in addition to the competitive aspect. I often go to tournaments, however, and witness instructors yelling, 'Kill 'em! Kill 'em! Break 'em up!' to their students, who then proceed to lose. I was a prime example of this. Fifteen years ago, if you'd lose, I wouldn't speak to you. It's not that I was that mean; I was *that* competitive as an athlete, and that competitiveness carried over to my coaching. But when I got into a structured program on a coaching level, I learned a whole different approach, a whole different philosophy of working to develop an athlete. I knew what it took to win (because I had won) and to train, but I didn't know how to *handle* an athlete. And that's something I learned about by getting into this program. You learn how to become a coach, a referee, a timekeeper . . . all aspects." Christina Muccini, a national karate champion three times as a junior and four times as an adult, and a bronze medalist in the Pan American Games, believes "an overzealous teacher can take a promising child and ruin it [the martial arts] for him, just because of the pressure to win."

## Competing Nationally and Internationally

Tokey Hill did not originally start off as a U.S. team member; he went from open circuit competition (which embraces all styles and includes tournaments that may or may not be under the auspices of an organization) to tournaments organized by the Amateur Athletic Union (A.A.U.), the National Governing Body (N.G.B.) of karate at the time. The N.G.B. is assigned to each sport by the United States Olympic Committee (U.S.O.C.), which is in turn recognized by the International Olympic Committee (I.O.C.). The National Karate-do Federation (N.K.F.) is the national governing body today; the international governing body for karate is the World Karate Federation (W.K.F.).

Examples of other organizations governing the martial arts are the North American Sport Karate Association (N.A.S.K.A.); the World All-Style Karate/ Kickboxing Organization (W.A.K.O.); the Amateur Athletic Union (A.A.U.); the United States Tae Kwon Do Union (U.S.T.U.) and the United States Judo Association (U.S.J.A.), the national governing bodies for tae kwon do and judo, respectively.

Judo, the oldest Olympic martial art sport, was introduced at the Tokyo Olympics in 1964. Tae kwon do was introduced at the Seoul Olympics in 1988 as a demonstration sport. Judo and tae kwon do are currently the only martial arts in the Olympics. If students are to develop from a junior Olympic level and eventually compete in the Olympics, they must be in the proper organization. However, students need not concern themselves with such affiliations in the early stages of training; young martial artists can still realize their potential by competing in  a variety of local and state tournaments.

"You can be involved in another organization," says Tokey Hill, "but in order to represent the United States in an official capacity, you have to go through the national governing body. You would have to go to their 'nationals' and their team trials. What makes it unique is that they have a grassroots program with structured training. The Olympic Committee has established criteria regarding training procedures, drug control, and so on, that one must meet in order to compete on the U.S. team. In addition, there's a code of conduct." The Olympic Committee is thus not only concerned with the competitive level of its members; it wants the United States to be represented with honor, respect, and discipline—which is what karate-do is all about.

Has this grassroots program developed a specific junior program, so a child can work his way up to a senior program? "Yes, it has," says Hill. "The hierarchy is as follows: local, state, regional, and then national. That's the program. Once you get past the regional level, you can qualify to compete on the national team. In the international community, they've already held a junior world championships in South Africa.

"Members of the junior team are seventeen and under; they are allowed to start at age ten. Every year, in Budapest, Hungary, there is a tournament. It's not classified as a junior world championships, but the international community regards it as such. Our junior program is called a grassroots program; it's similar to what has been done with gymnastics, ice skating, tennis, and all the other major Olympic sports, and it's purpose is the development of children to a senior level."

Although karate may not get the recognition it deserves in the United States, it is a world-class sport in all respects; in other countries, its champions are national heroes. Hill says that sport karate has increased his respect for traditional karate. "Just competing and getting to meet people from Japan and South Africa," he said, "really made me appreciate how the traditional aspect of training actually enhances the sport. It's much more structured, with many more rules regarding the scoring of points, but just to win, you have to have that traditional background; a person that does not, cannot win in this arena." He also stressed that in martial arts, as in anything else, "you have to progress with technology, or you'll be left behind."

## Beyond Fighting Skills

One of the most positive aspects of martials art as sports is that its "bad" practitioners are not turned away in favor of the "good" ones. In many other sports, and especially in team sports like baseball, football, and basketball, if you are not good enough to make the team, you're out; you are simply excluded from participating. No martial arts school, however, will turn away an unathletic or unpromising child whose parents choose to enroll him. As mentioned earlier, martial arts are essentially non-competitive, in the sense that there are no standards as to how rapidly a child must or even should progress. One competes only with one's self, and what is important is not how fast a child progresses, only that he progresses.

Students will, of course, receive belts indicating a higher ranking at different times. If a child remembers that he is in competition with no one else but himself, it should not matter to him whether he advances in a shorter or longer time than another student. He should also remember that learning faster does not always mean learning better. Achieving a goal and striving for excellence are most important, not the amount of time it takes to achieve the goal.

Now to answer the last two questions posed at the beginning of this chapter—Isn't the purpose of tournaments simply to develop fighting skills? If parents don't want their children fighting, what is the point of tournament competition? Training for tournaments and participating in them can improve endurance and overall cardiovascular conditioning; it can sharpen timing and reflexes; it can provide the experience of what it is like to get hit and valuable insight into how one might react to getting hit; and it can boost the confidence level of all those who participate, not simply of those who win. However, tournaments do not provide realistic "attack scenarios," nor an accurate indication of how anyone would fare in one. There is no direct relationship between freestyle sparring in organized tournaments and street fighting, and the former is not designed to imitate or serve as a substitute for the latter. Regardless, we can see from all the benefits we have listed above that tournaments are an excellent and beneficial component of martial arts training, and we highly recommend that all serious students of martial arts, when they feel they are ready, participate in them.

# PART III

*hapkido*

The characters for this popular
Korean martial art mean
"the way of coordinated power."

# THE CHILDREN SPEAK

*Teaching children is a gift, because you have the ability to make a difference in their lives by being a positive influence."*

—June Castro
eighth-degree black belt, shaolin kenpo karate

Our purpose in writing this book was to supply useful and practical advice to parents. To whatever degree we have succeeded, we still would have lacked, in our view, something in the way of authenticity had we not heard from the very people the book was ultimately written *for*—the kids themselves. To gather this information, we interviewed children of various ages and studying a variety of martial arts. We did not coax them, but merely asked them to respond in their own words to questions that adults might typically ask. To begin, we'd like you to meet Ryan.

Ryan is fifteen, has held a black belt for three years, and says that the movie *The Karate Kid* played a major role in influencing him to take up martial arts. He claims it has improved his health and physical well-being, and the way he thinks. He takes things one step at a time, and at a slower pace. He doesn't get overexcited, and, unlike the other kids, he doesn't get crazy about schoolwork and tests. He now tries to resolve things peacefully by talking them through; he doesn't blow his top as much as he did before taking up karate.

Ryan has never gotten into a fight. He has been confronted aggressively, but was able to walk away from it. If he hadn't taken karate, he might have punched the other boy. Because of his martial arts training, he is calmer and more confident, and this has helped him to keep situations from getting out of hand. He agrees that it's easier to walk away from a fight than to get into one.

In terms of a physical workout, he believes karate training is very well-balanced; in addition to helping him develop his upper body and legs, it is great for his entire body. These benefits, as well as his overall training, have helped him in other sports. His hip rotation, needed to swing a baseball bat with power, has been improved by karate training. On the basketball court, his increased leg strength has enhanced his jumping ability. About playing defense in basketball, he says, "If you want to trap someone, you can use your karate stances." In fact, Ryan once had a basketball teacher who was also a karate teacher, and who incorporated karate movements with basketball.

Regarding telling one's peers about his training, he says, "It's best not to advertise it, because a hot wire might want to challenge you." Asked what his message to other parents would be regarding letting their kids take up the martial arts, he replies, "Let them take it. They'll behave better, they'll learn to respect you, and you won't have to confront them as much, because they'll be more open about things they normally wouldn't tell you. They won't get into as many fights, they'll be more confident, and they'll walk with pride." To parents reluctant to permit their child to study karate, he would suggest they speak to the prospective instructor and to the parents of their child's friend who was studying karate. Ryan is a true believer. Karate has "molded me into the person I am today," he says.

Tara was constantly being picked on in school, so she asked her parents if she could take martial arts lessons. Now ten years old, she has been studying tae kwon do for a year and a half, and holds a green belt. Not knowing anyone at the martial arts school when she first started, and being one of the only girls, made her understandably scared. But now that she knows all the kids, and is comfortable with her instructor, she no longer feels this way.

Tara plays softball, and the punches she has done in tae kwon do have made her arms stronger. "I can throw and bat a ball harder," she says. In addition to sports-related benefits, she has also seen changes in herself. If someone laughed at her in the hallway at school, it used to really upset her. Now, she can say, "Forget about it," because situations like that are hardly worth her thoughts. She has more concentration, and can deal with things better. Like so many other kids, she singles out *The Karate Kid* as the martial arts movie she really liked. She also enjoyed *The Karate Kid II.*

Aditya is ten, and although he has been training in aikido for less than a year, his exposure to the martial arts began much earlier. "I had been taking tae kwon do for three years," he says, "and became interested in aiki-do. I decided to try it, and when I did, I found out it was a great martial art." He indicates, however, that he doesn't want to confine himself to one art. When he gets a black belt in aikido, he wants to continue on to study kung fu.

What, specifically, got him interested in aikido? "I liked it," he says, "because I saw Steven Seagal doing it in the movies. He's my favorite actor." He says that aikido, and the martial arts in general, has helped him a great deal. "I have more confidence," he says, "and I don't get scared if someone threatens me. It gives me discipline, and it teaches me to respect other people." Did his parents have reservations about him studying a martial art? "No," he says. "My mom said, 'Go for it!'

When we asked Aditya what he would say to another child and parent regarding studying a martial art, or aikido in particular, he was one step ahead of us. "I did that already," he says. "I told them that aikido is a very exhilarating martial art. If someone attacks you, you know how to defend yourself without seriously injuring the other person. They barely even touch you." Let's say a kid gets attacked, and defends himself [using aikido]. If someone comes along and says, 'What happened?' you can say, 'I was just defending myself.' If you kicked them or punched them, however, they'll probably think something else happened."

"Aikido is fun," he continues. "You do lots of rolls, and you learn how to fall without breaking your back."

Jesse is fourteen, has been training in tae kwon do for five years, and holds a brown belt. "I joined because I found the need to train in something," he says. "Tae kwon do was the first system that I came across. It looked as if it were a good system to learn how to defend yourself, and it was very athletic. I found it interesting, and I thought I'd try it and see how I liked it. I ended up staying, and I plan to stay longer."

Was it his idea to start, or did his parents coax him? "It was my idea," says Jesse. "I went to my parents first, rather than vice versa. "They always liked the idea of me trying it, and went right along with it from the start. In fact, my dad encouraged my sister to try it, but unfortunately she never did."

Jesse's instructor recalls that when he first started, at the age of nine, he was a very shy kid with no confidence, and poor motor skill development. Through his training and dedication, his motor skills have been greatly enhanced, and he has much more confidence.

Anthony is also fourteen, and has been studying karate for eight years. He got interested in it through watching his parents, both of whom were studying it. Although he loves sports, especially soccer and basketball, he was unable to participate because he had severe asthma. Karate was great for him, because it is an individual pursuit. His teacher tailored his instruction to Anthony's needs, and over the years, he has gone to a higher level than just a normal kid taking karate, and he has persevered in spite of his asthma.

According to Anthony, karate has helped him lose weight. He used to have minimal muscle strength, but now he's stronger, and can move and run faster. This, and the fact that he can now breathe easier, has enabled him to participate in sports. Recently, he has gotten involved in bowling. Karate has given him confidence and taught him discipline; he can easily walk away from a fight. He is selective in what he would tell people about his training in karate. When asked what he would tell parents who thought karate training wasn't safe, he said he would emphasize that when students spar, they use padding and gloves for protection. He would also tell them that students learn control and patience, and that a true martial artist never starts a fight.

Lindsay is fifteen and has been studying about six years. She told us she used to be very wild. Karate training has calmed her down, and taught her to relax. It has also helped her concentration in other areas, such as her schoolwork. "When I can concentrate," she says, "I can be the best I can be."

Currently a brown belt, she plans to test for her black belt in about a year. She feels she can actually defend herself. She doesn't think fighting is the answer, and has learned to walk away. Consequently, she has never gotten into a fight. She once talked her way out of a potentially physical confrontation: A girl in the locker room at school wanted to fight, but Lindsay said to her, "You really don't want to get into this situation." The confidence she exuded calmed the girl down and caused her to back off.

Lindsay's improved control has helped her tennis game. She used to get mad when she didn't make a shot; now, it's much easier to control her emotions. When asked to sum up her karate training in general, Lindsay thought for a moment. "It's something different," she says.

Jeremy is eleven, and has been studying aikido for under a year. He holds a yellow belt. Previously, he studied tae kwon do for two years. He wasn't happy with the system as it was taught to him in the other school, so his dad suggested he try aikido. He really likes it, and the "rolling" and "flowing" techniques appeal to him. In addition, he's happy with his instructor. "I really respect sensei," he says. "He helps you out when you do something wrong, and we're always focusing on the same thing for about a week; we keep at it until we get it right."

Does he think that aikido training can help kids in other sports? "Yes," he says. "It can help you to become faster. If you fall, you can get back up really fast. It can also make you stronger." Because Jeremy has not been studying aikido for a long time, he has not yet achieved the proficiency and spontaneity necessary to thwart a realistic attack. But even at this early stage, he practices in slow motion defending against punches and chokes. Undoubtedly, Jeremy will become extremely proficient, because he has the perfect attitude: We asked him how long he wanted to continue his training. "For the rest of my life," he replies. Is he interested in studying other systems? "No," says Jeremy, "only aikido. I want to become a sensei someday. I want to learn and teach other people."

What would he say to another child and parent regarding the martial arts, aikido in particular? "I would tell them it's great," he says. "It's a very good thing to do. You learn how to defend yourself in all kinds of different ways, not just in one certain way."

Bobby first started studying tae kwon do when he was five. Eleven years later, at he age of sixteen, he holds a third-degree black belt, and works as a junior instructor under his sensei. "The reason I ended up here," he says, "is that we moved here from another town, and my house was about three blocks away from the school." He singles out *The Karate Kid III* as the martial arts movie that really affected him.

Bobby has competed in quite a few competitions. "It's very interesting," he says. "You meet many people, and it's a lot of fun. I do get nervous sometimes; I look at my opponent, and sometimes he's bigger than I am.

But my instructor says, 'Don't look at their size; don't look at their rank; just do your best.'"

Has he been competing since the beginning of his training? "I started competing when I was ten," he says. "My parents didn't agree with the idea, because they didn't want me hurting somebody, or somebody hurting me. So I didn't compete until I was a red belt."

What are Bobby's views regarding fighting in the real world? "I would always walk away from a fight, even before I started studying tae kwon do. If someone is just saying something, I totally ignore that. I never pick a fight, but if fighting were my only option, then I'd have to be alert and ready for anything. During an altercation, I make a boundary around myself, a little circle. If they cross over it, I warn them first, but if they touch me, that's when I defend myself."

What advice would he give to parents seeking a suitable martial art and school for their children? "I think parents and their children should watch a class before they enroll, to see how the instructor treats the students, and to see if the students are comfortable in the class. If they are, and the instructors are very positive, give the kids compliments, and encourage them, then I think it's a very good school. As for a particular system, I don't think there's one system that's better than another. It depends how good you are in that system."

Daniel is fourteen, and has been studying karate for seven years. It was his decision, and he made it primarily to acquire self-defense skills. He has become more disciplined, and can react more spontaneously now; before he started training, he couldn't even block a punch.

Daniel's training came to his rescue when he encountered a potentially catastrophic threat. A man attempted to kidnap him, and threw a punch at him. Fortunately, his karate training enabled him to walk away unscathed. He saw the blow coming, and without even thinking, he shuffled away, smashed his assailant's knee, and threw a few strikes to his head. The attacker didn't even have a chance to get off another punch. Daniel exhibited what the goal of all martial artists should be: to react defensively without thinking.

Aside from his obvious ability to defend himself, karate has helped Daniel in physical education. He has gotten a lot stronger. Before he started, he couldn't do pullups; now, he can do many. In addition, his coordination is better. Daniel doesn't tell everyone that he knows karate. He feels that if the wrong person hears about it, he'll get into a lot of fights. The other reason is "because it's for me, and really no one else's business." He believes that developing the mind and spirit is as important, if not more important than the physical dimension of martial arts.

Michael is thirteen, and has been training for six years. The fact that he has only one kidney, located in the front of his body rather than in the back, was of concern to him and his parents when they decided he would take karate. He has to be very careful, but he views training as a means of protecting his kidney. Consequently, he's developed a great defense, as well as greater self-control and more confidence. The same focus he applies in his kata practice has carried over to his schoolwork, and it's helped him do better. He thinks it's best not to say much to friends about his karate training.

Michael is fortunate in that his father is an avid martial artist, currently preparing to test for black belt. In addition, his brother also trains. They all love sparring, and because karate is very much a family thing, Michael has lots of support.

Adam is ten, and has been training in aikido for four months. He got involved with it, because his friend Aditya told him about it. Prior to that, he had never heard of aikido. He was interested in the martial arts, however, since the age of three or four. He had seen it displayed in the movies by Steven Seagal and Chuck Norris. We asked him what he thought about his instructor. "Sensei?" he replies. "Well, he's the best instructor I've ever had in anything."

Has studying aikido helped him in other sports? "Yes," he replies. "If you're playing baseball, and the ball comes at your head, you can put your arms up. It's better to get hit on your arms than in the head. In soccer, if the ball gets kicked to your face, you could also put your hands up to block the ball." What Adam is saying is that the defensive maneuvers students learn to protect them from others, can be applied to other sports and other situations.

What would Adam tell a child or parent who expressed an interest in the martial arts? "I'd say, 'Go for it,'" he said. He also adds that if he were with another person, and someone attacked him, he'd defend this person. "And then maybe if he saw me doing it, he'd want to do it." What does Adam think are the most important things aikido will do for him? "It will give me confidence," he says "that if someone comes after me, I won't be scared. It will give me more discipline, and teach me to respect and help other people."

Joseph is fourteen, and studies judo. He had been interested in studying a martial art, and watched a few classes in various systems. Judo appealed to him the most; it also didn't hurt that the school was around the block from his house. He admits to being nervous at first, because he didn't know what was going on. "But I gradually learned," he says. "The instructors and students made it a lot easier. They were friendly, and welcomed me aboard." His sensei was the first martial arts instructor he had.

Joseph was five when he first started, and he trained for a year before leaving the school. As a tribute to his instructor—who not only was a great teacher, but one who cared personally for his students—he returned to the same school at the age of ten to resume his training. Now fourteen, he currently holds a blue belt.

Unlike the other children we spoke to, Joseph did not have self-defense in mind when he decided to study a martial art. "I just do it because I enjoy it," he says. "Judo gives you one of the best workouts you can get." How would he compare coaches in other sports with his instructor? "When I played baseball and basketball," says Joseph, "the coaches usually told us what to do, and we did it. Here, the instructor trains right along with us, such as when we're doing freestyle sparring.

Robert is twelve, and has been training for seven years; his brother Ryan trains, also. His father played semi-pro baseball, and Robert shares his enthusiasm for the game. His karate stances have helped his balance when he hits the ball, and because he's more flexible, he can run faster. Although a very small child, he has reached such a level of confidence that he's respected by all his friends. No one wants to fight with him, because of his confident demeanor. Consequently, he has never gotten into a fight.

Performing katas has helped his concentration, because "you have to focus a lot," and this has carried over to his schoolwork. Rituals such as bowing have taught him discipline, and his training has made him stronger. Robert will test for his black belt in about a year.

Tali is eighteen, and has been training for seven years. She and her friends had karate birthday parties, and she was also influenced by *The Karate Kid,* which she liked a lot. When asked what karate has done for her, she said it gave her discipline. Finding time for it was a problem, so she knew she had to get all her schoolwork done. It's helped her in sports: she's a lot more flexible, as well as stronger than everyone else. She's aware of what her body can do, what she can push it to do, and what her strengths and weaknesses are. Karate makes her feel more sure of herself, and she walks taller. "It's for me personally," she says; "it's not to show off."

Kevin is eight, and has been studying karate for four years. He likes it "because if someone comes up to me and starts hitting me, I know what to do." How did he know he wanted to do karate when he was four years old? "I had friends taking it," he says. Did he know what karate was at that time? "Yes," he says. "I saw it on TV." We asked him if there was a karate movie that he really liked, and he singled out *Sidekicks,* starring Chuck Norris. "I liked watching Mako teaching the young boy," he says.

Kevin's parents made the decision to have him take karate lessons. Did they have to convince him? "No," he says, "I wanted to do it." What has he learned about not fighting? "You shouldn't fight," he says, "unless someone comes up to you and starts fighting." Kevin plays soccer, and we asked if his karate training helped him in his soccer game. "It improves my kicking," he says.

As authors, we learned a lot from the kids we interviewed. For example, the specific benefits of martial arts study that they were able to apply to other sports and activities came as a revelation to us. Their words—infused with their own special brand of wisdom, humor, and honesty—perhaps constitute the strongest argument of all for the appropriateness of martial arts study for children.

# MARTIAL ARTS AND THE FAMILY

*This is what it's all about. We're instilling in these kids a sense of pride, a sense of wanting to achieve. And it all comes from martial arts philosophy.*

—Chuck Norris
world champion martial arts master and actor

Throughout this book, we've discussed the numerous benefits to be derived through the study of a martial art. Obviously, however, few children are able to pay for instruction entirely by themselves. This is why it is so important to us that the parents recognize the value of martial arts training. They will then view their children's lessons as an investment that will pay off for the rest of their lives.

In this concluding chapter, we hear from children who are studying a martial art, and their parents. Children and parents studying together would represent the ideal situation, but this is not essential. What's important is that the child has his parents' support and encouragement. The attitude should not be, "O.K., if you want to take up a martial art, go ahead." The parents should be involved in the process; they should go to the school to watch the classes, attend any tournaments the child may compete in, supervise the child's practice at home, and periodically discuss their child's progress with the instructor.

When progress is made (whether physical or behavioral), the child should be complimented. A compliment which is earned feels good, and encourages the recipient to continually strive to improve.

Daniel is sixteen, and first started taking karate when he was about six. Unhappy with his progress, he stopped after two years. About three years later, he resumed his training. His brother David, now twelve, had been studying for a couple of years. Seeing that David was doing very well, Daniel approached his brother's instructor and has now been studying shotokan karate with him for about five years. He currently holds a brown belt, and is very happy with his progress. Subsequently, Matthew, the nine-year-old brother of Daniel and David, started studying about two years ago. Currently an orange belt, Matthew says that his martial arts training has increased his concentration, which helps him in his schoolwork. It has given him better balance, better focus, better everything. "I just love it," he says.

David shares his brothers' enthusiasm. A talented soccer player, he represented the United States on a team that competed in a European tournament in Liverpool, England, in the summer of 1986. He has been studying shotokan for five years, and currently holds a brown belt. In addition to the many benefits to be derived by studying a martial art, David can cite one very practical one: the deep stances and kicking that he does in karate has increased his leg strength, and this has resulted in more power when he kicks a soccer ball.

The boys' mother, Edie, is very happy that her sons are taking karate. "I think karate has helped them focus, and has been great for their well-being in general. It's given them confidence, and it's given me confidence in them; I feel safer as a mother. When Daniel goes into the city, I feel better knowing he could defend himself if he had to. I think it's a wonderful release for them, and it really helps that they have the right kind of sensei. I found the group classes that Daniel was going to when he was younger to be more aggressive; they weren't representing the art of karate the way I felt they should. I think it's an art form, and it's very beautiful, but I also think it's clearly for self-defense, and shouldn't be used aggressively, because it can be dangerous."

What inspires Daniel to keep training? "The major reason," he says, "is that I want to stay in good shape. It's definitely a good workout, and it increases your confidence in all areas. I've never had to use karate in self-defense, but I have confidence that if I had to, I would be successful." We asked Daniel if he felt a child could be too young to study. "I think that kids at a kindergarten or prekindergarten age," he answers, "might not understand the psychological benefits, such as confidence, that can be gained. They won't view karate as a means of self-defense; they'll just see it as a way of fighting, which is not what karate is all about. So I think kids who are too young shouldn't take karate. A good time to start would be in the second or third grade."

Has Daniel become more assertive? "Definitely," says his mom. "He has grown very much as a result of his karate training; the confidence he develops in class is carried with him into all areas of his everyday life, whether it be in drama class, or practicing for a play. I don't think he would have tried out for the play he is in, if he hadn't been involved in karate."

Edie believes that the philosophy of the teacher sets the tone for the attitude of the children. "I really think," she says, "that a sensitive human being understands a lot of the pressures the kids are under, and this sensitivity will come out in his teaching. The respect the kids have for him comes from trust, and from knowing he really cares about his work and about them."

What would Edie tell other parents who were thinking about starting their child in a martial art? "I would tell other parents," she says, "that they really need to interview the particular instructor who's going to be teaching their child, and find out what his philosophy is. They shouldn't be afraid to ask a lot of questions. If the teacher's goals are in sync with theirs, then it's a good match." Edie also stresses, as does Daniel, the importance of watching a lesson, class, or classes before making a decision. "If the teacher is not open to this," she says, "that to me is a red flag. I observed the instructor before I hired him. If the instructor allows that, and you're happy with what you see, this can be very helpful in making your decision."

Would Daniel encourage a child or other teenagers to study a martial art? "Yes," he says, "but they definitely have to want to do it; I don't think it should be a decision that the parent makes."

Emily is twelve, has been studying martial arts for four years, and holds a brown belt. She initially got involved through her dad, who was taking lessons himself. Her father feels she has become more disciplined and more assertive. She loves going to the school and training. If she's upset, she soon feels much better. She was once given an assignment in school to write a paper describing a hero. She picked her instructor.

Emily once talked her way out of and walked away from a situation that might have escalated into a fight, because "they weren't trying to physically hurt me," but if they had been, she is confident she would have been able to defend herself. When asked what she would tell skeptical parents who were unwilling to allow their child to study karate, she replies, "I would tell them it helps you with everything. It teaches you respect and confidence, and how to defend yourself. It's also fun."

Fortunately, Emily didn't have to convince her parents. In the words of her dad, "It was very important to me. When Emily was born, I said I was going to take her for karate lessons. She always knew she was going to take karate." It's significant that Emily's dad not only took her to classes, but took lessons with her. "That got her into it, because we took it together."

Jacob is six and a half, has been training for two years, and holds a yellow belt; his brother Jared is eight, has been studying for four years, and holds a brown belt. Their mother Laurie got them into martial arts, because she thought it was "balletic without being 'sissy.' It develops strength and a lot of focus. I realized they weren't going to be the biggest kids in the world, and I wanted them to learn to look after themselves." Their father Harry says it teaches them great discipline and gives them a foundation for every other sport. "I got introduced to karate after Jared started," he says, "and I began to take classes about a year later."

We asked Laurie and Harry if they did any research before deciding upon a school and instructor. "I wanted to start my son at a certain age," she says, "because he seemed interested in it, and a lot of the local schools wouldn't take four-and-a-half-year-olds. They wanted them to be bigger, stronger, and older, so I only had a few choices. I had some friends that I trusted who had kids studying karate in a school that they really liked. So we went and watched first; then we started going there."

Jared first got interested in karate, because one of his friends was competing in a tournament. "I went with him and watched, and I wanted to do it too," he says. Before making her decision, his mother visited some schools, and was turned off by their emphasis on business. A lot of them were just interested in enrolling as many students as possible. They told her that if she paid a certain amount of money, her son could get a black belt. "You don't know if a four-year-old is even going to go to class tomorrow, much less what he'll be doing six years down the road," she says.

In addition to not requiring long contracts for years and years, she liked the idea that the classes in the school she chose would be conducted in Japanese. Jared's karate training has increased his leg strength. Consequently, his jumping ability while going for rebounds has improved his basketball game. "When I throw my punches," he says, "it makes my arms stronger, and I can swing a bat better when I play baseball. It also helps me feel better and stay focused."

Harry was asked what he would say to other parents regarding karate training for their kids. "I would tell them," he says, "to have their kids start as early as possible, not necessarily to get a black belt. I think self-defense is a good motivation, but to me, it's secondary. Karate gives you balance, and the foundation for everything else you need in sports. If you observe professional athletes, you'll see a lot of martial artists coming in to help them train after they've already developed, so it would be a huge plus if this could be done as they're developing."

Harry's uncle used his t'ai chi ch'uan skills to help members of the U.S. cribbage team "probably twenty years ago," he says, "and I just saw a program about the Pittsburgh Steelers. One of their top linebackers [Greg Lloyd] trains in martial arts, and I thought it was a great benefit to him."

"It's something they can start at a very young age," says Laurie. "You know that with boys, you're going to have a lot of athletic pursuits, so it can't hurt to be stronger, more balanced, and more flexible. My kids and husband are very flexible. They can put their legs over their heads, and karate helps keep them loose enough to do this. It keeps you able to do splits, twists, and turns in interesting positions, which is good for everything— basketball, baseball, football, whatever. You can start at any age, time, or level. It's not like a football or basketball team at school, where you're hoping everyone's the same. If you're willing to practice, you can reach a high level of accomplishment. I like it. It's discipline; it's focus; it's respect; it's another language. It has many rewarding aspects."

David is sixteen, has been training about six years, and is a third-degree brown belt. "Ever since I was young," he says, "I was into karate. My favorite movies when I was in third or fourth grade were *American Ninja* and *American Ninja 2.* I must have watched them three times a week for a long, long time. I loved Jean-Claude Van Damme movies, too. I liked the way martial artists in the movies carried themselves. They'd walk into a room, and didn't have to worry about anything; they knew they could take care of themselves. They always tried to avoid violence, but if they had to get physical, they'd be able to. There was a mystique about them; they always knew what to do and when to do it, and it was just automatic. They'd be really quiet, and could always hold back. But if there was a problem, they could take care of it; they could always turn it on." *Bloodsport* and *The Best of the Best* (about a U.S. tae kwon do team competing in Korea) were two movies that especially influenced him.

It was David's decision to start studying kenpo. When he approached his parents about it, they told him that if he wanted to try it, it was fine with them. A lot of people, however, told him he wouldn't stick with it. "You'll do it a little bit, get sick of it, and stop," they said. But David kept at it, because he enjoyed it.

"If I'm just play fighting in school," he says, "people realize that whenever they try to do something to me, I can always block it; I always end up with the upper hand." David was into water skiing, and wrestled a little bit. Kenpo helped him understand how to manipulate people's movements, and how to make them use their force against themselves.

Did he actually use kenpo when he wrestled? "Yes. I used a lot of the grappling techniques we learned. When my opponent and I would start off grasping each other,

I would drop my weight and cause his whole body to flip. I actually did this in a match." We asked David what changes he has seen in himself since he started training. "It's given me more confidence that I could protect myself. I might not be able to protect myself in every situation, but I have a certain confidence that I have a much better chance with it than without it."

What would he say to a kid who was thinking about studying a martial art? "I would say to try it, because you'll love it. It will change your whole life, and it will teach you to be a better person." What would he say to a parent who asked him about martial arts for his or her child? "I would tell them that what I like best is the whole culture and philosophy behind it. I would also tell them to make sure the teacher stands for something, not just money. They should tell kids not to fight if they don't have to, and that if you can walk away, you should walk away."

Jan is David's father, and we asked him what his reaction was when David wanted to do martial arts. "I thought it was a wonderful opportunity for him, because I felt the martial arts would teach him discipline and make him stronger, both mentally and physically. In this day and age, it's important for a child to be able to defend himself, too. All in all, I viewed it as a 'win-win' situation. As it turned out, I believe his training has made David a better person."

What is Jan's overview as he looks back on the six or seven years of David's karate training? "I think it's a wonderful discipline for children," he said, "and it's very important. It takes a lot of time, it's a challenge, and it's physical, so they're building their bodies; it's a mental challenge, so they're building their minds. David is always thinking about what move he's going to make next. There's a lot of memorization involved, and an understanding of concepts and principles is important. It's more than just moving your arms around; a certain amount of philosophy is taught. I think the martial arts makes kids more confident and secure, and I hope David sticks with it a lot longer.

"To other parents, I would say that if their child has any kind of inkling toward doing it, he or she should do it. I think it's a wonderful thing that they have the self-confidence to know that in a particular situation they will walk away, because they feel confident they can take care of themselves. And if they have to defend themselves, they have the ability to do so. I think this is something that's important for every kid."

What would Jan's advice be to other parents regarding finding an instructor or school? "I don't think you should just go to a school," he says. "You have to talk to people who have either worked with the instructor or attended the school. It's like anything else you want to do. The school might look beautiful; it might have a nice carpet on the floor, but that doesn't mean it's a good school. If a kid stays interested and focused and is learning what he's supposed to, that's more important than what the place looks like, or where it's located.

Jan recently watched David compete with a weapons form in a tournament. "You see people of every size, shape, and ethnic background," he says. "But they're all out there doing the same thing, and trying to win. It just proves that it's the kind of activity that could be popular with everyone; it's not confined to a particular type or class of person. It's really for anybody that wants to learn it, as long as they put the time in."

Did David notice something in common with everyone at the tournament? "They all had respect for each other's style and system," he says. "The fact that you bow to show courtesy," interjects Jan, "indicates there are certain things you do which are standard and consistent. They all know about discipline and respect, and that's what karate is all about."

If a child is studying a martial art he shows an interest in, likes the atmosphere of the school he goes to, is comfortable with the instructor, and has the full support of his family, the many benefits can enrich all aspects of his life. This is the message we hope to impart. But only you can take the suggestions, and turn them into positive action. Getting started is usually the hardest part of any new activity, and the foolproof cure for procrastination is, "Do it now!" Do not be discouraged if your child does not seem happy at first. This does not necessarily mean that the martial arts are not for him. He simply may not be comfortable with a particular school, instructor, or system. Use the suggestions in this book, and with a little work, you should be able to find a school and instructor he is happy with.

In conclusion, we urge all children to turn the key, open the door, and enter the world of martial arts. Over the threshold lies the start of a wonderful journey, a road to inner strength, self-awareness, and a more peaceful and satisfying life.

# FURTHER READING FOR KIDS (AND PARENTS!)

Festa, Tom. *The Adventures of Martial T. Holiday, Nos. 1, 2, and 3*. Franklin Square, New York: Kamase Publications.

Greenburg Baker, Carin. *Karate Club, No. 1, Fight for Honor*. New York: Viking Children's Books/Puffin Books, 1992.

—. *Karate Club, No. 2, High Pressure*. New York: Viking Children's/Puffin Books, 1992.

—. *Karate Club, No. 3, Road Warriors*. New York: Viking Children's/Puffin Books, 1992.

—. *Karate Club, No. 4, Girl Trouble*. New York: Viking Children's/Puffin Books, 1992.

—. *Karate Club, No. 5, Out of Trouble*. New York: Viking Children's Books/Puffin Books, 1992.

Millman, Dan. *Quest for the Crystal Castle*. Tiburon, California: H. J. Kramer, 1992.

—. *Secret of the Peaceful Warrior*. Tiburon, California: H. J. Kramer, 1991.

—. *Way of the Peaceful Warrior: A Book That Changes Lives*. Tiburon, California: H. J. Kramer, 1980. (For teens and adults)

Webster-Doyle, Terrence. *Facing the Double-Edged Sword: The Art of Karate for Young People*. Middlebury, Vermont: Atrium Society / MAPA, 1988.

—. *Fighting the Invisible Enemy: Understanding the Effects of Conditioning.* Middlebury, Vermont: Atrium Society / MAPA, 1990.

—. *One Encounter, One Chance: The Essence of the Art of Karate.* Middlebury, Vermont: Atrium Society / MAPA, 1997. (For teens and adults)

—. *Tug of War: Peace Through Understanding Conditioning.* Middlebury, Vermont: Atrium Society / MAPA, 1990.

—. *Why is Everybody Always Picking on Me?: A Guide to Handling Bullies.* Middlebury, Vermont: Atrium Society / MAPA, 1991. (For teens and adults)

# ABOUT THE AUTHORS

Richard Devens is a writer and a classically trained pianist with a B.S. and M.M. in music performance. He has long had an interest in the martial arts, and is a student of kenpo. Although music and the martial arts are seemingly disparate endeavors, he feels they share more common elements than may be readily apparent.

Norman Sandler was introduced to judo in 1967, at the age of thirteen, and later wrestled as a member of his high school team. He studied kenpo karate under the supervision of senior grandmaster Ed Parker, who personally tested him for all black belt levels up to fourth degree; he now holds a fifth degree. In 1975, he commenced *goju-ryu* training, receiving his black belt in 1979. Undertaking shotokan training in 1977, he became a certified J.K.A. (Japan Karate Association) black belt, and as captain of the United States National Karate Team, he won gold, silver, and bronze medals in international competition. In 1984, he was introduced to the Filipino martial arts, and continues to train in *kali*. Believing that one must "give something away to keep what one has," he has been teaching martial arts, with an emphasis on young children, since 1977.

Mr. Devens and Mr. Sandler have collaborated previously on articles appearing in *Kung Fu, Official Karate, Karate/Kung-fu Illustrated, Dojo,* and *Black Belt* magazines. Both authors welcome questions and comments from readers, which may be sent to them care of Weatherhill, Inc.

The "weathermark" identifies this book as a production of Weatherhill, Inc., publishers of fine books on Asia and the Pacific. Editorial supervision: Ray Furse. Book and cover design: D.S. Noble. Production supervision: Bill Rose. Printing and binding: Quebecor, Inc. The typeface used is Veljovic, with Futura for display.